Community Mental Health
A Study of Services and Clients

Community Mental Health

A Study of Services and Clients

Donald H. Miller
University of Washington

Lexington Books
D.C. Heath and Company
Lexington, Massachusetts
Toronto   London

Library of Congress Cataloging in Publication Data

Miller, Donald H
  Community mental health.

  1. Community mental health services—Utilization. I. Title. [DNLM:
1. Community mental health services—Utilization. 2. Health and welfare
planning. WM30 M647h 1974]
RA790.5.M54   362.2'2   73-11653
ISBN 0-699-89425-7

Published simultaneously in Canada.

Printed in the United States of America.

International Standard Book Number: 0-669-89425-7

Library of Congress Catalog Card Number: 73-11653

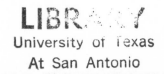

To Harold V. Miller—
a pioneer in American
urban and state planning

Contents

List of Tables
and Figures

Acknowledgments

Thanks are gratefully given to a number of people who have extended assistance during the preparation of this book. Various staff members of San Francisco Community Mental Health Services, and especially of Westside Community Mental Health Center, Inc., went out of their way to facilitate collection of the data on which the latter half of this study is based. Dr. Barbara Blackwell Polos, in particular, was instrumental in securing access to the data and in helping to unravel many of the problems which inevitably occur as records are gleaned for information.

Professors Douglas B. Lee, Jr., Roland Artle, and Michael B. Teitz, at the University of California, Berkeley, were generous with their time in reviewing earlier drafts of this manuscript. Their helpful criticisms and continued encouragement were very important to the outcome of this project. My thanks go as well to Marge Smart, for an excellent job of typing several versions of a difficult manuscript. Many others, too numerous to mention, in one way or another have given me encouragement or have helped shape my ideas. I hope that I have personally acknowledged their assistance. I, of course, accept responsibility for the flaws remaining.

Community Mental Health
A Study of Services and Clients

1

Introduction

Community mental health care is a relatively recent addition to the several human resource services which are publically provided in response to socially recognized problems and developmental opportunities. Governmentally financed outpatient care is intended to make mental health services available within residential communities, thus reducing reliance on distantly located state hospitals.

Additionally, localized provision of psychiatric care is intended to assist in identifying and treating mental disturbances in their early and less acute stages and to make psychiatric services available to all citizens. Delivery of this service has taken a number of forms, and much of the variety observed among programs is the result of deliberate experimentation, but little is actually known about the impacts of these alternative designs.

This study investigates how community mental health services for outpatients are used, and how their use by the psychiatrically distressed could be increased by changing various features of the way in which these services are provided. Empirical work is based on records for outpatients using services provided by Westside Community Mental Health Center, Inc.—a consortium of agencies serving the residents of a public health district which includes approximately one-fifth of the population of San Francisco, California. Data collected for this research include the demographic characteristics of, and services received by, 1,305 clients first admitted during five sample months from 1968, 1969, and 1970.

Knowledge of the ways in which various groups of consumers regard and use a public service such as outpatient mental health care is important to the process of designing the service in a manner which is responsive to consumer desires, and which will encourage desired patterns of utilization. The research on which this book is based began as an inquiry into ways of improving the spatial distribution of supply locations for various public services, with relation to the intended consumer population. It soon became apparent, however, that locational considerations could not be separated from other features of the delivery system for any public service without overly simplifying the analysis. Concentration solely on locational issues would foreclose considering innovations in service delivery which could yield higher returns in terms of utilization than would an improved locational strategy alone. Conseqently, a more systematic approach was developed for viewing consumer behavior and for analyzing the impact of supply on utilization. Outpatient mental health care was chosen as the specific type of service to investigate.

1

In summary, the major objectives of this inquiry are:

1. To identify and analyze the major variables accounting for consumption or utilization of community mental health services for outpatients supplied at a set of locations within the urban area.

2. To investigate the relative importance of these variables in influencing consumption behavior, and the manner in which these variables differ in importance for people from various sociocultural groups.

3. To contribute toward developing a methodology for evaluating alternative plans for locating and providing community mental health services for outpatients such that these services will be used in a manner which is consistant with the intentions of public policy.

Overview of the Issues

Evaluation of systems for providing public services has normally stressed the process involved in producing these services. With the advent of cost-effectiveness analysis, attention was broadened to include the extent to which these services meet explicit public objectives.

A major rationale for public provision of a service is that use of the service generates benefits to persons other than the direct consumer or, in other words, that the service is affected with externalities of consumption. Subsidized provision of a service may also be used as a means of redistribution for purposes of achieving greater social equity.

In each of these two cases, consumption should be viewed as a part of the process involved in generating the public good as well as the private good elements of the public service, hence in attaining the objectives of the service. Yet it is in the consumption portion of this process that public service systems such as outpatient community mental health care commonly fail. This failure is indicated by their underutilization by those publics for whom they are intended.

Economic theory of consumption reasons that an individual's willingness to consume a commodity or service is largely influenced by that individual's assessment of the net benefit which will be derived from the act. This net gain is a function of the individual's anticipated satisfaction from consumption, balanced against the various monetary and convenience costs which will be incurred as a result of consuming that service.

Response by consumers to varying prices permits some analysis of the demand for market goods. Public services, either provided without direct user charge or at a subsidized price, pose greater problems in analysis. These problems are in addition to those arising from the external nature of some of the benefits derived from consumption. Consumption behavior with respect to public services, however, appears to parallel that for market goods, permitting cross-application of some of the findings from studies of consumer purchasing behavior.

It is reasoned that consumer responses to a program of outpatient community mental health services are influenced by various characteristics of that program—characteristics pertaining both to the facility and to aspects of the service provided at the facility. Accessibility, or inversely trip-making costs to users, is one of several interdependent variables which together appear to influence consumer behavior. Consequently, it is posited that analysis of alternative locational strategies for providing outpatient mental health services must jointly consider the influence of variables such as familiarity with the service and attitudes toward the convenience and amenity of using the service once the point of supply is reached.

Research into the spatial behavior of people making shopping trips and into their consumption behavior further points out that these variables influencing demand differ in importance to consumer groups with different characteristics. These intergroup differences may be expressed as weights to the several variables influencing behavior. The combination of these variables, their group-specific weights, and the manner in which these variables are related specify a consumer-demand function for the service. Development of such a function would facilitate evaluating a set of similar alternative proposals for providing the service, in terms of the implications of these proposals for consumer behavior.

The facilities and activities constituting a mental health program form a hierarchy, ranging from the most specialized and nodal inpatient and rehabilitation services, to more general and dispersed outpatient and public information services. With the use of drugs in modern therapy, psychiatric care has increasingly come to involve short-term hospitalization, partial hospitalization, and outpatient care.

A current trend in providing psychiatric care is to relate facilities and services to localities, reducing the need for removing patients from the context and life of their community. The emphasis of this study is on factors influencing the utility and use, from the consumer's point of view, of the most local or decentralized of these facilities. These are the outpatient clinics of various sorts, which provide direct patient care, evaluation along with admission and referral services, and commonly indirect services such as public education and consultations to agencies and community caretakers.

Approach of this Study

The strategy used in this investigation is to review, synthesize, and extend work which has explored the role of accessibility and other supply characteristics of mental health services in influencing consumer behavior. This material provides a basis for developing a number of hypotheses, which are tested with data on consumer behavior that was assembled for this study.

Chapter 2 provides a critical review of previous empirical work. While very little reported research has treated mental health services, there is a substantial body of literature analyzing the provision of somatic health services. Much of this research has focused on some of the effects of distance on demand for health care. Few examples have been found which attempt to deal systematically with the consumer's decision process in selecting and using a set of health services.

Chapter 3 investigates the general origin of demand for outpatient care, and seeks to answer the questions: What is mental health and illness? What are some of the causes and means of treating psychiatric problems? What are some of the forms which mental illness takes? Recent governmental programs and reorganization of psychiatric services, in response to the increasingly recognized problem of mental illness in this society, are also discussed.

Chapter 4 discusses the sources of public concern and interest in providing mental health services. Here, answers are sought to questions such as: What is the nature of the benefits generated by the provision and consumption of the service? How and why does the service differ from those typically considered as market goods, thus encouraging public intervention?

These chapters provide the framework for the empirical work, which is presented in the second half of this book. In Chapter 5, the services and organization of the Westside Community Mental Health Center are described, and the social organization of the Westside District population is investigated. Analysis of client data reveals that the frequency of patients coming from some residential areas is greater than from other residential areas which are closer to the agencies providing the services.

Chapter 6 examines who uses outpatient services and how they enter therapy. Among clients first admitted during the sample months used in this study, women are found to outnumber men, and young adults are the predominant age group. While black clients are more frequent than expected on the basis of population figures, other studies suggest relatively high rates of mental illness among people with low income such as many of these residents of the Westside District. Consequently, it appears that black people, as well as members of other racial minority groups, are underrepresented among the clients of these outpatient services.

The way in which people are referred to outpatient services also appears to vary on the basis of group membership. For example, many black and Mexican-American clients are referred by hospital clinics and similar medical services. Physicians and social service agencies are less frequently cited as sources of referral than was anticipated. These and other findings are useful in designing programs to improve the information of counselors and prospective clients.

Chapter 7 reports on extensive analysis of the influence exercised by physical access on consumer behavior. Frequency of use declines as the distance between places of residence and conventional outpatient clinics increases, but use increases with distance from the Crisis Clinic, the only source of short-term care. Similar patterns are found for discharges, as opposed to premature withdrawals, for these two kinds of services. Black and Mexican-American clients are found to be extremely sensitive to increases in distance from outpatient clinics, but their proportionate use of the Crisis Clinic substantially increases with distance.

Physical access appears to be only moderately important in explaining variation in consumer choice of the clinic to patronize. Chapter 8 presents analysis of other supply characteristics which influence demand. Differences between the kinds of services provided by the Crisis Clinic and by outpatient clinics account in large part for differences in consumer behavior. The Crisis Clinic is the admitting agency for one-third of the white patients and for two-thirds of the black and the Mexican-American clients first entering therapy during the sample months representing 1969 and 1970. Outpatient clinics are found to differ among each other in their attractiveness as sources of service on the basis of such characteristics as intake procedures, reputation for quality of care, community attitude toward the agency, pricing policy, and popular information concerning the availability of therapy.

While analytical findings reported in this study identify factors which exercise important influence on consumer behavior and demonstrate intergroup differences in response to these factors, we still do not have adequate information for client-oriented planning. Chapter 9 outlines a promising approach for future research. Recent work by other investigators seeks to further abstract features or characteristics of service packages which affect the ways in which various consumers evaluate the opportunities available to them. A hypothetical formulation of a consumer response model is developed. This model has heuristic value for further analytical work and could provide a method for evaluating the design of service delivery systems, when more is known about the influence of supply variables on consumer behavior.

2

Factors Influencing Consumer Responses in Utilizing Health Care Services: Theoretical and Empirical Studies

Design of public services in a manner which takes consumer tastes and perceptions into account has become a topic of increasing concern among urban planners and other professionals over the last decade. Economic efficiency in organizing services has begun to be tempered by interest in making services available, acceptable, and accessible to the clients for whom these services are intended.

Early spokesmen for the urban planning movement in the United States stressed the desirability of providing public services that would be attractive to the residents of cities.[1] Standards suggesting acceptable levels of capacity and location for public facilities represented the major methodological approach used by professionals in developing planning proposals. These standards, in addition to being of dubious origin and validity, tend to preclude testing alternative plans or proposals.

During the late 1950s, some urban planners began to discuss a new, client-oriented approach to developing proposals for public action,[2] thinking in terms of public services instead of solely in terms of public facilities,[3] and developing methods for ascertaining the desires of various groups of citizens.[4] Dominant concern for developing and applying knowledge of various consumer or client groups and their interests in formulating public policy and action has been identified as one of the major current paradigms of planning.[5]

Martin Meyerson has been credited with playing a major role in developing the current user-oriented approach to urban planning. Meyerson had concluded that planning was irrational because its proposals were usually incongruent with the goals it was ostensibly serving; and that the widely used planning standards were primarily implementing the goals of suppliers.[6] These notions were the premise for a study in which Dyckman, Meyerson, and Gans sought to identify the purposes and behavior patterns of various actors connected with particular institutions. These actors included the suppliers, the users, and the community, including political decisionmakers.[7] The questions of what the goals of various actors are and how these goals should be ranked "are political of course, but they ought to be answered systematically as well as democratically, and no one has yet invented a viable method to complement the politicians' *ad hoc* solutions."[8]

Gans eloquently sums up the definition of *planning* which emerged from this study:

Unless there are good reasons to the contrary, planning ought to be user-oriented

7

and ... public priority determination ought to be compensatory wherever possible, so that the members of a community which obtained the least resources from the private sectors of society ought to obtain the most from the public sector. Few of our basic ideas were original, and today, they have become almost commonplace in planning, at least in its lip service.[9]

In a brief treatise on public libraries, Gans provides an illustration of a strategy for user-oriented planning.[a] Starting with a client-centered conception that an institution "ought to cater to the needs and demands of its users,"[10] he suggests that by studying consumer behavior "it may be possible to infer practiced objectives."[11] *Clients* are defined as those publics which a service or institution affects, "either functionally or dysfuncitonally." Two strategic principles which he infers are that an institution (a) should serve a specific set of clienteles, mainly those not served adequately by other methods of distributing the service, and (b) should serve the people who live within the "range" of the service; the distance which people will travel to obtain that service.[12] Consumer research in a specified market area becomes a major methodological device for pursuing user-oriented planning.

Application of information concerning consumer behavior and preferences in planning for the location and design of public services requires a systematic definition of how these services operate and are used. In laying the groundwork for developing a needed theory of public facility location, Teitz examined theory from several complementary fields for possible contributions.[15] He found that public economics could facilitate a classification of services based on the nature of the goods provided, and analysis of geometric characteristics of where services are consumed supports a broad classification on the basis of point-supply or delivered services. Distribution of demand and supply begins to suggest the effects of decentralization of economics in distribution, while the notion from central place theory that agencies or facilities form a hierarchy providing differentiated sets of services is a useful partial explanation for observed spatial patterns.

Teitz formulated a static system model, using as his criterion the total consumption of a service.[16] He identifies consumption of a service as a simple function both of the scale of service centers, thus presumably the quality or variety of specific services provided, and of the number of centers at which

---

[a]Client analysis and orientation has not widely influenced planning for health services. An extensive survey of health planning reports concluded that a potential category of information for health-care planning is examination of patient attitudes toward available health services, personal use of current facilities, and opinions about health care. Only two of the plans reviewed touched on these topics.[13] Publications on planning specifically for mental health delivery systems have focused almost exclusively on the range of services to be offered and organizational arrangements for providing these services. Little more than passing mention is made of where and how or in what particular forms these services should be provided. The desires or predilections of various groups of consumers, if recognized at all, are treated almost as an afterthought, and then in extremely general terms.[14]

services are provided, which implies the dispersion and accessibility of supply points. The consequent normative model seeks to maximize consumption subject to a budget constraint.

While the model appears only partially to account for observed variations in consumption behavior, it does constitute a first approximation of this process. The realism of this formulation would be increased by substituting a function of several variables characterizing the service and the manner in which it is delivered for the simple size variable. Similarly, more analytical treatment of distance would account for several sources of cost to consumers in reaching the service and the relative importance of these costs. Finally, the estimating accuracy of such a demand function, when applied to a heterogeneous population, would be enhanced by separately assessing demand for each of several groups of consumers with similar tastes and behavior. Disaggregation in this manner would, as well, support distributional analysis; that is, assist in understanding the differential impact of proposals on various clienteles.

These recent developments in planning thought and principle provide the conceptual framework for this study. The following sections of this chapter narrow the discussion to theoretical and empirical health-services research into consumer responses to variations in supplying health care. While our major interest is in factors influencing the choice and utilization of outpatient mental health services, most reported research deals with medical services, and especially those supplied at hospitals. Because of the similarities between mental health and medical care, both in terms of the natures of producers and processes and in terms of popular conceptions of the services, the full range of health services research has been reviewed.

For purposes of this discussion, factors influencing consumer behavior have been grouped into three classes. The first of these is the effect of accessibility, as measured in several ways. We will see that the role of physical distance is a dominant concern in this literature. Secondly, we will deal with the impacts of client characteristics on consumer behavior. Finally, we will analyze findings concerning the influence of service or institutional characteristics on the way in which people choose and utilize health services.

The Influence of Distance Variables on Consumption Patterns

Distance between the client's place of residence and the hospital or other point of supply of medical care is the most frequently examined variable in health-services research which deals with patterns of consumer behavior. There are several reasons for this. Most studies dealing with factors influencing consumer response depend on patient records. Because patient records almost without exception include home addresses, these records accommodate use of some measure of distance. Secondly, distance measures are usually considered as among the most objective variables available to consumer-demand analysis. As the following critical analysis suggests, this may be illusory. Finally, measures of physical distance are effectively the only continuous variables for typifying observations in investigations of disaggregated and distributed demand analysis. This also constitutes a major reason for the exceptional attention shown to physical distance in the literature concerning the locational behavior and spatial structure of human activities.

A widely used methodological approach to identifying problems and developing proposals concerning the delivery of health services examines supply and demand within a delimited area. The spatial unit used may be a study area, or alternatively a catchment or service area commonly established for administrative purposes. Ratios of resident population to available beds, local physicians, or other indicators of supply are estimated and compared to ratios held to represent acceptable or desirable levels of service.[17] Use of such an area approach is thought to indirectly evaluate accessibility.

In addition to the problems inherent in most standards used in planning for public services,[18] the service or study area approach has additional shortcomings. It assumes that all people have similar needs or demands, and that all sources of supply or units of health-care service are perfect substitutes, or are equally regarded by the consumer. Secondly, the service area approach assumes the existence of monopolistic market areas or hinterlands for each point of supply. This condition seldom holds; the distribution of clients for a hospital, for example, tend to spatially overlap similar distributions for other hospitals within a metropolitan area.[19] Finally, spatial definitions of study areas usually do not correspond with areas having ecological meaning, with the consequence that summary figures obscure differences between individuals and groups within an area and disparity in their access to health services.[20]

For these reasons, research has turned increasingly toward analysis of individual behavior and the role of distance in influencing patterns of utilization. Distance has been differently defined as straight-line and most direct route by available roads. Distance has been measured in physical units, total effort including availability of private automobile or public transport and conditions of connecting roads, and in terms of travel time. Some recent discussion has suggested using subjective or perceived travel time as the most realistic typification of trip-making effort. The following discussion identifies the major health-services research dealing with distance and the prominant findings of these studies.

Physical Measures of Distance

Probably the earliest investigation to consider the impact of distance on health-care consumption was the work of Lively and Beck in 1927.[21] Their observation that medical care utilization in rural areas decreased with increases in distance between consumer and the physicians supplying the service. This finding was reenforced by other studies of this period.[22]

It was almost twenty years before health service research again analytically investigated the effect of distance. Dealing with rural residents in Missouri, Jehlik and McNamara found a decrease in the rate of physician visits and more days of bed illness with increasing distances between patients and doctors' offices.[23] They also observed that the impact of distance on demand for preventive services was relatively greater than for therapeutic services, and that sources of supply located in frequently visited activity centers were the most frequently utilized.

These conclusions were further supported by Ciocco and Altman, who found that the frequency of trips by rural residents to physicians was relatively high under five miles, declined sharply with distances in excess of five miles, but became relatively constant with great distances.[24] Computing a regression coefficient representing the "friction of distance," they observed that the frequency of visits to a general practitioner varied inversely to a value between the square and the cube of the distance traveled. Analyzing utilization of several types of medical services, they found smaller distance exponents or flatter distance decay curves for specialty services than for general medical service.

While this was interpreted as showing that clients would travel further for specialized care, the relatively greater distances traveled also probably reflected the increased centralization of these kinds of services and possibly the demand inelasticity with respect to distance for specialized medical services. Centralization of specialities was described by Weiss, who found that metropolitan population concentrations and the related location of medical centers explained observations of disproportionately high numbers of doctors to population for physicians in medical practices such as surgery.[25]

Physical measures of distance have also dominated recent efforts to deal with the impact of accessibility on consumption and choice of medical care suppliers. Investigating demand patterns in metropolitan Chicago, Morrill and Earickson found that in selecting physicians, "patient reaction to distance, determined from actual behavior, is one of indifference up to about two miles, after which attractiveness falls off rapidly" in an exponential manner.[26] This initial range of indifference to distance is comparable to the zone of maximum competitive advantage, a notion developed by Golledge in spatial market analysis.[27]

Analysis by Weiss and Associates of client selection among three clinics supplying prepaid health care in Portland revealed that proportionate use of the closest clinic for most common services declined with increasing distance.[28] Of course the difference in distance to the next nearest clinic commonly declines both absolutely and proportionately as distance to the nearest clinic increases, which may in part account for their results. Their analysis fails to account for variables such as other client activity patterns, especially work and shopping trips, differences in past use patterns including habituation of patients in using the central clinic, or differences in the size or perceived quality of the several clinics. In short, distance appears to influence consumer choice, but in this case it is not shown to be "a strong determinant of which clinic is utilized."[29]

Intervening variables such as trip purpose appear to affect the impact of physical distance on consumption. For example, Schneider found that people traveled slightly further for inpatient psychiatric service than for general medical service provided by hospitals and considerably further than for most medical services.[30]

Morrill and Garrison, in analyzing data for Cedar Rapids and Seattle, identified the greater "range" or distance which people will travel for medical care than for most other services and the willingness of clients to travel further for specialist than for general pratitioner services.[31] They reason that this behavior is a function of the importance attached to a particular doctor or service, and the great concentration of facilities and physicians.[32] These conclusions are reinforced by Morrill and Earickson, who found that distance decay curves for larger and more specialized hospitals derived from the residential distribution of current patients were flatter for larger and more specialized hospitals than for smaller, general service hospitals.[33]

Income, or race when it is found to be a reliable indicator of income, has been identified as another intervening variable. On the basis of their analysis, Morrill and Earickson found that choice of hospital by black people differed from that for whites, and that the role of the physician in the choice by black clients was best accounted for by substituting the mean of the hospital distance from physician and from patient for simple distance from patient.[34] These examples of intervening variables are complemented by a fuller discussion of client and service characteristics which follows.

Several studies of the disparity between the distribution of demand and the location of supply have used simple physical distance as the measure of accessibility. Early in a series of papers on this topic, Cherniack and Schneider used straight-line distances from centroids of postal zones to hospitals in calculating the median center or "point of minimum aggregate travel" for all patients going to each of thirteen hospitals in Cincinnati.[35] The direction and distance between this computed point and the current hospital location is taken as an indication of current locational inefficiency. While they observed "barrier effects" of natural and administrative boundaries, they failed to deal with the time-distance effects of freeways, for example. Elsewhere, Schneider notes that accessibility has monetary-cost and time-cost dimensions, but justifies his use of straight-line distance with a citation of the report by Lowry on the high correlation between over-the-road and airline measures of physical distance.[36] Applying the approach just described, Schneider concludes that centers of demand were about two miles distant from points of supply.[37]

These several efforts to calculate the spatial center of current demand grow out of two studies which attempted to optimize between production economies of large scale or agglomeration, in this case for teaching hospitals, and travel costs both for delivering supplies and to the staff and clients incurred by concentration.[38] A complementary normative model has been developed by Earickson, who first allocates patients by community of residence to physician clusters or to hospitals, using a modified gravity model.[39] Next, patients are shifted from physician clusters or hospitals of excess demand until demand is equalized, or alternatively capacity is shifted from locations of underdemand to locations of current overdemand in a manner which minimizes the aggregate distance traveled by clients. The greater aggregate distance required by shifting patients, or the travel saved during one month by decentralization and relocation of services, is used to calculate current locational inefficiencies.[b] Earickson found, for example, hospital capacity shifts in response to the existing distribution of demand in Chicago would result in a 20 percent average reduction in patient travel.

Time and Cost Measures of Distance

A second major approach to dealing with accessibility and its impact on consumer behavior involves replacing physical distance with a time or cost measurement of distance. Shannon and associates make the point that the major source of resistance to trip making is the total effort involved, and that this is only approximated by direct measures of physical distance.[40] They suggest that travel time is a more appropriate measure of effort, but that it overlooks familiarity with the route, multiple purpose trips, and perceived or subjective travel time.

One of the earliest efforts in health research to use travel time was a study to develop locational proposals for eight major hospitals providing specialized medical services to the population of Sweden.[41] The objective was to minimize aggregate travel time and travel cost to the predicted distribution of population. Six existing facilities in major centers were accepted as given, two new facilities were located, and service areas were delimited. The method used was to construct isochrone-maps presenting time-distance by one-hour increments on the basis of the availability and operating characteristics of various transportation modes. Boundaries of service areas were drawn where the same time figures from two centers met.

In the United States, federal guidelines for planning hospital locations have encouraged consideration of available transportation and travel time,[42] and the impact of new freeways in changing the time-distance to various locations has

---

[b]The criterion of efficiency, rather than equity, presumably was both more simple to specify and more politically acceptable.

been discussed, though in general terms, by several articles dealing with satellite hospital location.[43] However, the first research along these lines in this country appears to be that reported by Morrinson.[44]

In this project, driving times from various Cincinnati hospitals were measured by five-minute intervals. The resulting equal time areas or isoquants replaced simple linear distance circles in defining approximate hospital service areas, demonstrated the importance of freeway construction in changing accessibility, and when analyzed with data on population distribution showed that one-third of the people living in the region were within twenty-five minutes of a hospital complex.[45] An especially interesting finding was that newer suburban households are no further from older central hospital locations, in terms of time-distance, than older centers of population located physically nearer to the central hospitals.[46]

Analysis of patient origin data for ten hospitals in Santa Clara County, California, led to the conclusion that travel time is a more meaningful measure than road distance in explaining choice and use of these hospitals.[47] A computer mapping technique was used to measure the minimum travel-path time from the population centers of census tracts to the available general hospitals in the county. It was found that 90 percent of all inpatients had residential locations within fifteen minutes of the hospital used, and that the average time-distance was less than ten minutes.[48] A rapid dropoff was noted in the percentage of patients going to each specific hospital with increasing auto travel time, but the study showed no differences in attenuating effect of travel time among three major categories of medical service. This unusual finding may in part have resulted from the high level of supply of hospital services suggested by the low average time-distance figure.

Weiss and associates state that analyzing the effect of distance or access is more complicated in studies of metropolitan areas than when dealing with fairly separated places.[49] Morrill and Garrison concur, stating this as one of their research conclusions.[50] Regardless of the context, physical distance appears to be of limited use, and travel time a better measure of the cost as perceived by consumers. "Human involvement in terms of effort, the distribution of effort over multiple purposes, choice between alternatives, and the ease of transportation" become some of the features which factors representing distance should reflect.[51]

Social Structuring of Space

Our discussion to this point has dealt with the impact of distance on the utilization of health services. Implicit in such discussions is the unimportance of another dimension of spatial analysis—the role of place or the particular location of a service in influencing effective demand. This is a highly questionable assumption, since most locations have social meaning for residents of an area.[52] Thus, for example, a Catholic hospital would not likely be built in a Jewish neighborhood, or a private psychiatrist to locate in an urban ghetto. Hägerstrand states this in other words as he notes that when the individual is dealing with space, he deals not only with distance but as well with territories; his conceptual organization of space into sharply bounded areas.[53]

Empirical work with territories in health-service research has been extremely limited. One reason for this is that reliable data is difficult to obtain and use with the same ease that measures of physical distance can be analyzed. Yet recent work by social geographers and others has pointed up the importance of individual and group perceptions of the environment in influencing spatial behavior.[54] In response to the findings of these researchers, Earickson notes that, "traditional theories of location and interaction now appear somewhat obsolete . . ."[55,c]

The perceived environment of greatest consequence to the individual is commonly referred to as one's social or action space. Wolpert has defined action space[d] as the area with which the individual has contact and within which most of his activities take place.[57] Formation of one's action space is affected by the individual's group membership, position in social networks, age or position in a life cycle, and spatial location relative to potential trip destinations, principally the place of residence.[58] Physical definition of an action space may include discontinuous or separated areas, and may be modified with changes in the age and socioeconomic status of the individual.[59] While such mental maps are based on each individual's experience, these images are in many respects held in common by groups of people with similar socioeconomic characteristics and occupying the same area.[60]

Residential neighborhoods have, in some contexts, been referred to as the social or action space of occupants.[61] However, a study which controlled for variations in the size of the area defined as the neighborhood found that locally recognized boundaries were not by themselves an effective basis for predicting the location of many common activities pursued by residents.[62] Analysis of the spatial distribution of household activities of various socioeconomic groups has demonstrated both intergroup differences in spatial behavior and that action spaces usually extend beyond neighborhood boundaries.[63] These studies suggest

---

[c]Similarly, Downs makes the point that deterministic location theory frameworks commonly assume away much of the cognitive process in human decision-making. Alternatively, a cognitive behavioral approach focuses on the nature of the decision-making process and on parameters affecting its outcome. A fundamental parameter is the type and amount of information about the environment which is available to the individual, as well as how this information is structured and evaluated. Down's empirical work identifies nine cognitive components or characteristics of a downtown shopping center from which individuals construct their image of the opportunities which the center provides.[56]

[d]*Ambience* is a similar term used in several empirical studies to denote the spatial arena of frequent interactions.[64]

that realistic action areas are usually larger than immediate residential neighborhoods.[e]

In the health services literature, Morrill and Earickson deal with the relative location of hospitals, finding that the proportion of patients close to, and cared for, by a hospital increased with its size and isolation.[65] This gives limited support to the notion that action space influences the choice of hospital. Lindheim identifies the role of familiarity in encouraging utilization.[66] Corcetti and associates make the point that familiarity with individuals who have been mentally ill and visits to people in psychiatric treatment will reduce resistance to seeking assistance for personal problems.[67] While these studies relate to the work by social scientists on the role of perception in spatial behavior, they remain somewhat peripheral to the subject.

Earickson, in attempting to apply these concepts to utilization of health services, considers simultaneously the psychosocial and economic aspects of the spatial behavior of hospital patients in the Chicago metropolitan area.[68] He argues that the patient views trips to a physician or hospital both in terms of his action space and how he expects to be received at his destination.[69] For example, the patient will be more willing to choose a destination which is within his action space and will tend to restrict his social ventures in search of medical care to those offices or hospitals where he perceives that his status is high. Thus, in racially and ethnically homogeneous areas of cities, there is much more social movement within the area than outside of it.[70]

Earickson identifies several social variables influencing human spatial behavior and interaction, thus modifying the effect of physical distance.[71] Poverty is commonly associated with previous nonurban life experience which reduces the social space of poor individuals, and the more affluent seek to avoid the poor, including segregating their institutions such as hospitals. Religion, while less influential in defining social space than in the past, is a basis for residential clustering and several religious groups support hospitals which provide religious functions. Race is a prominant basis of residential and health-care discrimination, which extends to black physicians and limits the hospitals to which their patients can be referred.[72] Ethnic minorities such as individuals strongly identifying with their country of origin or ancestry also have distinctive social spaces usually as a matter of choice. Members of these minorities usually prefer doctors from the ethnic group, and commonly maintain their own hospitals. Age, as noted earlier, effects action space and position in a life-cycle influences the residential location of families.

---

[e]An additional term, *social distance*, is sometimes used in an aspatial sense to mean differences between the values of an individual and those of a social group or organization which are perceived as great enough to make rejection or lack of satisfaction from interaction highly likely. Hall (*The Hidden Dimension*) uses the term as a psychological notion to describe physical distances beyond which a person feels anxious in attempting various types of interaction. While social distance may be best used in dealing with the degree of compatibility between individuals and groups, when these occupy space the resulting relationships can be mapped and clearly effect spatial behavior.

The series of studies developed by the Hospital Planning Council for Metropolitan Chicago and published as technical reports collected substantial empirical evidence supporting the importance of action spaces as influencing the supply and utilization of medical services. However, substantial problems were encountered in designing a method for systematically analyzing the effect of action spaces on consumer behavior and in isolating this effect. A method used involved developing a matrix of weights which represented the "race-religion compatibility" of hospitals and patients.[73] These were applied to physical distances to provide a measure of effective social distance. We will return to a discussion of this technique in this chapter's subsection, "Race and Religion."

Intervening Opportunities and Competition

The treatment of accessibility in health services research, especially when distance is viewed in terms of physical separation or travel time, usually adopts a gravity model framework. Interaction of clients with a hospital is seen to be an inverse function of distance, with the measure of distance usually raised to a power.[74] As will be seen later, several studies have investigated the direct relation of hospital size on consumer behavior.

Recent research has adapted elements of Stouffer's intervening opportunity model.[75] Statistical analysis of flows between communities and hospitals in Chicago were found to be approximately equally influenced by the size of demand and measures of hospital size, as suggested by the gravity model, and by the inverse of the amount of intervening demand and opportunities.[76] The first of these latter two variables is defined as the intervening population closer to the hospital than to the sending community.[77] This appears to be an indicator of competition for service at a hospital. Intervening opportunities were defined as hospital beds closer to the community than those supplied by the receiving hospital. This provided a measure of alternative sources of the service being sought. Underestimation of many large flows was attributed to referrals which, because of institutional arrangements, disregarded a number of hospitals more highly accessible to patients.[78]

Some findings of research using Cincinnati data appear to support the appropriateness of using an intervening opportunities approach. Cherniack and Schneider observed that intermediately located hospitals acted as partial barriers to patient travel.[79] However, Schneider found that points of minimum aggregate travel for patients using particular hospitals were located further than similar points for some intermediate hospitals.[80] While this would suggest that some intervening hospitals are not perceived as real alternatives, the institutions demonstrating greater drawing power may be providing nonequivalent services. Differentiation of hospitals on this basis will be discussed more fully in a later section.

Physician Referral and Hospital Distance

Spatial accessibility, variously defined, has been seen to affect consumer behavior in selecting and using medical services. However, the discussion to this point has dealt only with the separation of the medical service from the location, usually the place of residence, of the consumer. While this appears to be reasonable in the case of medical care supplied by a clinic or physician, it is an oversimplification when the medical care is supplied by a hospital.

The role of the physician in influencing the behavior of individuals concerning the sources and types of medical services consumed has received increasing attention in the general demand literature of the last two decades. The physician operates in a manner somewhat similar to a firm in combining components of care, the inputs of medical service, to produce a service, in this case a treatment.[81] While the physician is expected to choose these components on the basis of their efficacy and relative prices to the patient, he is constrained in doing so.

These constraints include institutional arrangements, especially in referrals to those hospitals with which he has a staff appointment; the extent of his knowledge such as concerning the effectiveness of substitutions among components of care; and sanctions such as the activity of review committees which examine the admissions and length of stay for the patients of each physician.[82] Also, the physician acts in his own interest, as well as the patient's, in choosing components of treatment which will protect his practice and economize on his own time and effort.[83]

Thus the physician is involved in determining the demand for hospital service and usually decides for the patient which hospital will be used.[84] Unlike market goods which the consumer chooses directly on the basis of available information and personal evaluation, the consumer choice involved in utilization of hospital services is commonly limited to the selection of a physician.[85]

A Cincinnati study mentions the role of physician in hospital selection.[86] Earickson develops supporting evidence, finding that for all patient-to-hospital trips in Chicago, physicians and hospitals are usually closer to each other than either is to the patient (47 percent).[87] The second most common pattern is for physician and patient to be closer than either is to the hospital (27 percent), while only the third most common pattern is for patient and hospital to be closer than either is to the relevant physician (17 percent). The most common context of the latter case is where older hospitals occupy central city locations and the supply of physicians in poorer central areas is inadequate.

Morrill and Earickson noted the major importance of physician intervention between patient and hospital, but were unable to incorporate this into their regression models of patient flows.[88] Their later simulation model took the role of the physician into account by employing the strategy of allocating patients to hospitals using the mean distance to various hospitals from the physician and patient.[89] While this model is reported to have yielded acceptable results, it is clear that the problems of dealing with the role of the physician in hospital selection have yet to be fully resolved.

Approaches to Dealing with Spatial Distributions

In concluding our discussion of studies treating the impact of accessibility on consumer behavior, it is important to mention several techniques which have been employed to measure the spatial distribution of demand. These techniques are major tools for analytically dealing with patterns of consumer movement in utilizing health care. They also may be used in determining field-of-attraction models for structuring catchment areas for hospitals and in evaluating the impact of new hospital locations on aggregate client travel and demand for services.[90]

Linear measures have included demand-density curves[91] and time-distance isoquants to calculate likely patient movements and service area overlaps.[92] The direction and distance of a vector from a hospital location to the point of minimum aggregate travel of its patients has been used to demonstrate what the authors refer to as the existing locational inefficiency of the hospital.[93] Use of a standard deviation ellipse has been explored as a means for reflecting the planar spread of a spatial distribution such as demand for a point supply good.[94]

Greater analytical detail is facilitated by developing sectorgrams of two-dimensional distributions.[95] To construct a sectorgram, the mean locational points[f] and major axis of a spatial distribution of demand are calculated, eight sectors centered on the principal axis are then layed out, and the standard distance[97] for each sector is used as its boundary. Comparison of such a sectorgram for all patients and sectorgrams for patients of each hospital may be used to suggest appropriate locations for additional or reallocated service capacity.[98]

Efforts to further refine distributional analysis have resulted in a three-dimensional analogue model which permits a graphic display of qualitative and quantitative data on the same base map.[99] In a comparison of this approach with the ellipse and sectorgram methods, the authors concluded that the latter tended to "conceal both the clustering and radial associated patterns which are evident in the three-dimensional distributions."[100] While the approaches using standard deviations can oversimplify distributions, they do provide useful summary statistics.

The Influence of User Variables on Consumption Patterns

Several investigators have recently cited demographic characteristics such as age,

---

[f]The mean locational point is defined as the point of minimum aggregate travel.[96]

sex, race, income, and other social characteristics, along with proximity, as "controlling variables" in explaining frequency of use and selection of health services.[101] Yet there is little agreement about the relative role played by these various factors. Modeling efforts find it necessary or seductively convenient to omit most client characteristics in analyzing demand for health services.[g] Additionally, there are few examples of research which have chosen the alternative route of disaggregated analysis, standardizing for social characteristics to account for behavioral differences between client publics. The purpose of this section is to identify and discuss the findings of reported health-service research which does deal with consumer characteristics or patient variables.

Race and Religion

Race and religion have been treated as operating in a similar manner in influencing patterns of consumer behavior. Solon and associates interviewed a three-month sample of outpatients at Beth Israel Hospital in Boston, identifying each patient's characteristics and asking about the sources and relative importance of various health services which they used.[103] They found that subcultural groupings of patients had distinctive patterns of obtaining hospital outpatient medical care.

Further analysis of this data showed that similarity of the ethnic identity of patient and hospital increases consumption at that hospital, a feature which Solon identifies as "cultural identification with source of care."[104] Variations in demand, associated with ethnic and other sociocultural characteristics, should be accounted for in making decisions concerning, for example, physical provisions, staffing arrangements, procedural mechanisms, and information and communication systems.[105] Solon concludes that receptivity to sociocultural diversity will influence the quality of care, both from the patient's point of view and probably in effectiveness in securing a cure.[106]

Earickson classifies the patient population of Chicago into four groups: those preferring hospitals with Jewish, Catholic, or Protestant direction and physician staffing, and black patients.[107] These "compatabilities" between client and organization are based on dietary and other social customs in the case of religious affinity,[108] and on bias and exclusion in the case of race.[109] Statistical regression analysis using Chicago data showed that patient flow from a residential area to a hospital was greater when racial or religious similarity between hospital and community existed than when the two were dissimilar.[110] In developing a simulation model of hospital use, Earickson's classification of clients was expanded to six categories including the three religious groups,

---

[g]Similarly, plans for health delivery systems seldom discuss population characteristics and the consequences of these in terms of the appropriateness of services to be provided.[102]

black-paying, charity, and white-paying religiously indifferent.[111] Allocation of each group to hospitals was done separately, and compatibility was dealt with in terms of effective distance, which is essentially a physical transformation of social distance as defined earlier. Model calibration suggested that on the average, for example, Jews evaluated the distance to non-Jewish hospitals as about three times further than to Jewish hospitals, while Catholics and Protestants evaluate dissimilar hospitals as about twice as far.[112]

Income, Occupation, and Social Status

Income or ability to pay for medical service is highly intercorrelated with race and with education and occupation, which are common bases for social status ascription. Because of their close and complex relationships, these several variables will be discussed as a group.

General revealed demand or the quantity and quality of medical care consumed is widely recognized to be largely a function of income. [113] Some have suggested that this relationship between income and total family consumption is approximately linear.[114] However, it has been demonstrated that incidence of somatic illness is inversely related to income.[115] In other words, demand for care in large measure reflects ability to pay rather than need for care.[116] Mental health similarly appears to be positively related to income (see Chapter 3's section, "Some Exceptional Features of Demand for Mental Health Services")

In terms of consumer choices among suppliers of health care, most analysis has dealt with differences in distances traveled by members of different income groups. One study does note that the lower the status job of the head of the patient's household, the greater the dependence of the patient on a community supported hospital outpatient department for medical services.[117]

Bashshur and associates found that white people, or those with higher average income and education, travel further for physician services than do nonwhites or persons with less education and income.[118] This finding probably results from a combination of conditions mentioned earlier; that higher income persons face lower cost and inconvenience from travel, that they possess better information and exercise greater selectivity in their choice of physician, and that they live in suburban locations while physicians and particularly specialists tend to cluster in the vicinity of medical centers.

Bashshur also reported, however, that less than 7 percent of the sample studied used the physician nearest their residence. In other words, the decisions of most health-care consumers can not be explained by distance minimization alone. Analysis of choices among clinics in a prepaid health-care program similarly showed that while distance played a role, social status had little effect on the tendency of patients to use the nearest clinic.[119] Finally, in analyzing patient flows from relatively small subdivisions of Chicago to various hospitals, a number of client and hospital variables were found to be significant, however, "income or education levels as such added little explanation."[120]

In summary, it appears that income and other status variables play a very large role in the amount of medical services consumed, but that these same variables have not successfully explained where this service will be sought. Reports on efforts to analyze the structure of consumer behavior in light of these variables are too incomplete to identify methodological problems which could have influenced these results, but covariation with other social characteristics may partially explain these findings.

Age and Sex

As with the preceeding set of client characteristics, age and sex clearly influence the general level of demand for medical services, but less clearly affect the choice of where these services will be sought. For example, Feldstein reviews the literature showing that as individuals age, the incidence of illness increases and increasingly frequent causes of mortality are accidental injuries amd chronic diseases.[121] He also points out that the relationship between age and revealed demand for medical care is not a simple linear one.

Similarly, Ro found that the aged have longer hospital stays than do younger members of the population.[122] Concerning source of supply, Solon notes that choice of hospital outpatient services as opposed to those of private physicians increased with the age of the patient, if clients less than fifteen years old were omitted.[123]

Women are found to incur greater expenditures for medical care than do men, mainly as a result of obstetrical charges.[124] Consequently, demand analysis must consider age, sex, and marital status in combination. However, Ro found that females had the same average length of hospital stay as males when childbirth was omitted from the analysis.[125]

Age does have an effect on the spatial behavior of individuals.[126] Our earlier discussion of the social structuring of space made the point that one's mobility and action space is a function of experience and independence which in turn are affected by the individual's position in a life cycle.[127] Using three age categories, Weiss and associates found that proportionate use of the clinic nearest the client's place of residence declines with age, apparently largely as a function of multiple purpose trips for work and other activities, but that sex was not an important explanatory variable.[128]

Finally, Morrill and Earickson note that the number of residents sixty-five years or older was a significant variable in explaining patient flows from a community to particular hospitals, especially when accounting for the absolute number of medical-surgical patients from a community.[129] The regression power coefficient in this case was the largest of those for eight variables used ($1.238, r^2 = 0.651$). While our preceeding comments suggest that the number of people aged sixty-five or older is an indicator of general demand based on incidence of morbidity, its use in the equation shows it to be more powerful in explaining choice and use of hospital services than the variable dealing with distance or variables describing characteristics of the service.

The Influence of Hospital or Service Variables on Consumption Patterns

The third set of variables affecting consumer behavior in selecting and utilizing medical care represent the characteristics of the service offered by various agencies. These are supply variables but, unlike distance or location, are features of the good or establishment available at a particular site. From the consumer's vantage point, these characteristics are a major basis for evaluating the relative attractiveness of alternative opportunities for obtaining health care.

Switching perspectives, a service establishment such as a hospital has a drawing power, the strength of which is a function of not only its accessibility, but also the casemix and special clientele it may seek to serve, and what Schneider has referred to as "attractiveness factors."[130] These latter variables include quality of medical service, prestige, and level of nonmedical amenities. As Schneider notes, each of these are important to both the physician who is usually involved in the referral and to the patient.[131]

A major problem with several of these variables is the difficulty of measuring them. Yet, in light of this probable influence on consumer behavior, any effort to explain this behavior as it is manifest in terms of demand for services at various agencies must somehow take these variables into account. It is our purpose in this section to identify and discuss supply variables which have been dealt with in health-services research.

Size of Hospital or Service Center

Several measures used to typify the size of an establishment supplying medical care such as a hospital or clinic include number of staff physicians, number of nurses or interns and other staff, and number of beds, which is sometimes multiplied by occupancy rate to give a measure of the availability of capacity.[132] The size of a medical office center is commonly measured by the number of physicians in a cluster.[133] While the number of beds available at a hospital is highly correlated with the scope of services provided,[134] we will deal with the availability of special medical services separately.

The scale of the hospital is widely held to be a major variable in accounting for the volume of demand from a resident population. Interpreted as a measure of "size of opportunity," one study reasons that people view a larger hospital as a better one, and varyingly substitute size for distance.[135] Elsewhere, number of beds was found to be a significant variable in multiple regression models of absolute and proportionate flows of patients from communities and for a model of a hospital's proportion of medical-surgical patients coming from a community.[136]

Graphically, the slope of the distance decay curve for frequency of patient trips to particular hospitals in Chicago, differentiated primarily by size, was found to be steepest for the smallest and least for the medium-sized competitive hospitals.[137] These results are in contrast to findings in Cleveland, where attractiveness as measured by the rate of decline in demand with increasing distance was observed to be about the same for hospitals of various sizes.[138] The Chicago findings tend to be corroborated by a French study, which concluded that size and complementarity of two or more clustered hospitals gave the best results as measures of attractiveness for allocating demand to hospitals in medium-sized cities.[139]

An interesting feature of hospital size as a factor in influencing demand is that institutional size also appears as an important variable in increasing the economy of production.[140] Hospital construction and equipment has become increasingly and exceptionally expensive over the last two decades. Demand for specialized facilities is often of such a nature that these facilities must serve a very large population if they are to be used at reasonably high levels relative to their capacity.

As discussed earlier, the prospect of efficiency from large-scale production has encouraged researchers to develop a maximizing approach involving tradeoffs between hospital size and consequent centralization, and the increased travel costs incurred in service and use of the hospital.[141] Currently, too little is known about these effects to successfully analyze alternative proposals in a rigorous manner. Further, it is questionable whether mental health services can realize economies of large-scale production comparable to those attributed to medical-surgical hospitals.

Concerning choices of doctors for office visits, the number of physicians in a cluster was reasoned to be a measure of attractiveness representing capacity and probability of satisfaction for purposes of constructing a simulation model.[142] Elsewhere, Morrill and Earickson report on empirical evidence that the number and variety of white physicians in a cluster is the best measure of attractiveness for that cluster to white patients. Black patients were found to respond similarly, visiting both white and black physicians, though showing some preference for the latter.[143]

Physical Amenities

Physical amenities probably have an effect on consumer demand in a manner similar to the effect of size. All else being equal, a new and well-decorated hospital or clinic would tend to be preferred over its less physically attractive counterparts. Various income groups may respond to this variable differently. The greater expenditures for medical care by higher-income families appear in part to be for the purchase of greater comfort.[144]

Physical amenities are often considered in analysis of shopping behavior, but do not appear explicitly in health-services research. One study does employ a variable which may be an indicator of environmental quality in classifying hospitals.[145] "Recent dynamism" is a factor score derived from changes in size and admissions over a fifteen-year period and the age of the hospital. It is noted that the dimension is important because clients appear to prefer newer hospitals.

Capacity and Crowding

The capacity of a service, and the consequent availability of medical care to additional clients when demand is at a given level, is a variable closely related to the size of the institution. Our discussion of size as a factor in attractiveness noted that measures such as number of beds or staff were sometimes multiplied by occupancy or treatment rates to yield a measure of capacity.

Just as crowding or pressure for beds at a hospital will shorten the average length of stay of patients,[146] excessively high occupancy rates will tend to cause a hospital or other medical institution to reduce admissions, and long waits for admission will decrease the attractiveness of a hospital or agency to a patient and his doctor.[147] Feldstein points out that increases in bed supply affect the relative cost to a physician for providing care; that when physicians are busy they will tend to substitute hospitalization for their own time in treating patients.[148] The reverse also probably holds.

In explaining under utilization of some hospitals, Schneider discusses in general terms the notion of occupancy pressure; observed occupancy rate minus a normal occupancy rate.[149] He suggests that occupancy pressure is not only a function of proximity to market and size of market, but relative attractiveness. This would suggest that hospitals with high occupancy pressures would continue to be pressed by excess demand, if available competitive facilities remained constant and their reputations as desirable sources of service continued. Attractiveness may be diminished when admission requires excessively long waits, but no studies of this effect of congestion have been reported in the health-services literature.

Morrill and Earickson indirectly treat crowding or competition for capacity by using available data on intervening demand, or the population between a residential area and a hospital, in their simulation models of patient flows.[150] They find that flows are consistently related to the inverse of intervening population, and that this variable along with intervening beds as a measure of alternative opportunities accounts for 40 percent of the variance. While occupancy rates are among the variables used in deriving factor scores for the purpose of classifying hospitals, these rates were not analyzed for their effect on consumer choice of hospitals.[151]

Quality or Level of Services

The range of facilities or number of medical specializations have been used in several studies to differentiate between hospitals offering partially different outputs. The more complex the output or specialized the case, the greater the average cost per patient is likely to be.[152] Patients will also tend to come greater distances for specialized care because their condition is usually more serious,[153] and because hospitals closer to their place of residence are not able to provide these services.

Levels of services provided by various hospitals, based on the specializations which they offer, have been used to define hierarchies of hospitals. Schneider developed a three-level hierarchy in a study of Cincinnati hospitals.[154] Morrill and Earickson defined a hierarchy of five hospital classifications, but were required to estimate levels of service from the number of facilities and data on services in which interns or residents were involved.[155] The number of facilities was found to be a significant independent variable for each of several models for predicting flows of patients to hospitals.[156] The flow between a community and a hospital is reduced as the number of facilities at the hospital increases, since specialized care centers serve wider spatial distributions of patients, primarily the more difficult cases.

Elsewhere, analysis of consumer data revealed varying patterns of distances traveled for different kinds of hospitals.[157] For example, the proportion of patients living close to, and cared for by, a hospital increases with size and spatial isolation but decreases with the number of medical specializations offered.[h] On the other hand, the rate of decline in demand with distance is least for research or special purpose hospitals.[i] Hospitals offering higher level services appear to have a monopoly in supplying care for many kinds of cases.[159]

A study using sectorgrams to analyze the residential distribution of patients for various hospitals in Cincinnati supports these conclusions. Comparison of sectorgrams demonstrated that different classes of hospitals had markedly different "types" of service areas, with teaching and research hospitals having

---

[h]By way of illustration, major research hospitals had a long mean patient distance (8.9 miles) and a low mean distance exponent (0.5), whereas medium-sized hospitals were found to have shorter mean distances (4.1 miles) with little variability, and much steeper slopes of decline of use with distance (mean exponent 1.06).[158]

[i]These characteristics of demand have been reflected, in a largely *ad hoc* manner, in the location of branch hospitals. Branches are subordinate units of a single system, with certain functions available only at central locations.[162]

the broadest distribution of demand.[160] Yet an earlier analysis of patient data for this city failed to find any consistent variation in the slope of spatial demand curves related to the scope of medical services provided by hospitals.[161]

Policies and Type of Control

Policies of hospitals and other sources of medical care often act to limit the individual's range of choice, and consequently strongly influence consumer behavior. A number of publically financed health services are administered on a spatial basis, with the requirement that the client be a resident of the political unit or health district in order to qualify.[163] In such cases, employment or other activities may then require individuals to make special scheduling arrangements and lengthy trips for these services. Relationships among health agencies and institutions, both in coordinating the provision of services and in making referrals, can operate to reduce these constraints on consumer choice.[164] Ginzberg argues convincingly that a district basis for regionalizing health services is more desirable than a citywide or metropolitan basis.[165]

Linkages between health agencies and other public and private social agencies which are accepted by a population can also lead to consumer acceptance and use of a health service.[166] Policies concerning the hours during which clinical services are available have been found to have a significant effect on their use, especially if these hours conflict with the schedules of intended clients.[167] Similarly, policy favoring experimental programs, local participation in policy-making and management, and deliberate use of paraprofessionals can increase the effective utilization of locally provided services such as clinics.[168]

Special medical programs affecting consumer choice take several forms. Prepaid programs limit clients to choosing among clinics or hospitals operated by the program.[169] Available medical care for the poor is in part supplied by charity institutions, which are commonly administered by county or state governments and are often far removed from the homes of patients. Some charity institutions are overcrowded and are notorious for their indifferent service. Yet these agencies are often the only source of service available to the medically indigent. A third form of special medical program is financial assistance for the poor through local welfare funds, or more commonly by medicare and medicaid. Even with these assistance programs, the poor often find it difficult to locate a physician or hospital which will accept the program in admitting them, and they frequently receive patronizing treatment.[170]

As mentioned earlier, acceptance of blacks or members of other racial minority groups operates to restrict these consumers to relatively few of the medical institutions located in an urban area.[171] Controls consist of admissions policies, which are increasingly under legal attack, and less overt social pressures such as expressions of hostility which discourage future efforts to use the particular agency. Similarly, black physicians are limited in their affiliations with hospitals, which in turn limits their referrals.[172]

Overt and covert racial constraints on access to medical institutions are so pervasive that, for example, a Chicago study adopted the analytical technique of allocating blacks only to those hospitals known to accept them, then allocating them to the nearest available hospital. The difference in total distance traveled was interpreted as a measure of the cost imposed on this group by these existing constraints. It was found that open admissions would decrease aggregate travel for black patients by 16 percent.[173]

Price and Source of Payment

Out-of-pocket expenses are recognized by most studies of consumer behavior to be a major component of trip costs, and the reasoning employed is that the choice of the medical institution to utilize will be affected by the relative distances to available alternatives. Yet few of these studies deal with the prices of services obtained, and the effect of differing prices on the source of supply which is chosen.

General demand studies such as those by Klarman[174] and Feldstein[175] discuss the effect of prices and income on the decision to seek medical care and the amount consumed once treatment is undertaken. Feldstein also points out that net price, that is the actual out-of-pocket expense incurred, and the perceived amenity or quality differences in units of service which account for some variations in price, should be considered in demand analysis.[176] Investigation of consumer behavior in choosing among suppliers of a medical service becomes quite complicated when these corrections are attempted.

For example, choice among hospitals should standardize for characteristics of the services sought. One study showed that patients at hospitals with medical training programs stayed longer and paid more than at hospitals without these programs.[177] This would suggest that hospitals without training programs would be more attractive on the basis of price; however, the more expensive sources of care are larger and more complex hospitals which are usually sought when a medical problem is complicated or especially serious.

Net price, while difficult to calculate, can in part be dealt with by examining the source of payment. Four major categories of patients by primary source of payment include: government, free service, insurance, and patient. This listing is in the order of diminishing use of hospital care, at twenty-two institutions in western Pennsylvania, and amount of care is positively related to the total bill.[178] If a hospitalization is a transaction unit, intended to effect the cure of an episode of illness, then this finding reflects the price sensitivity of hospital use by the consumer. The client who pays out-of-pocket uses the service least, whether or not he secures the full benefits to regained health realized by longer-term patients.[j]

Source of payment is known to be important in explaining patient flows to various hospitals.[180] For example, hospital acceptance of charity patients is a group specific constraint affecting the availability and relative attractiveness of service. Morrill and Earickson found that simulation of patient movements to hospitals required them to allocate charity patients separately, based on known capacities of hospitals to care for these patients.[181] Charity patients were also found to go directly to hospitals, without physician referrals. If current arrangements restricting poor patients to a very few hospitals were removed, it was found that these consumers would save a great deal in travel distance required to secure hospital services.[182]

Other special groups such as those with veteran status who consequently have access to veterans hospitals and prepaid group members who must use hospitals operated by the program can account for portions of patient flows to a set of hospitals on the basis of source of payment.[183] Yet data on even these components of total demand for medical services are usually difficult to obtain. Although recognizing the importance of source of payment on consumer behavior, Morrill and Earickson found that these variables could not be meaningfully incorporated into their statistical model.[184]

Summary and Conclusions

It is apparent from this review of the theoretical and empirical work dealing with consumer behavior regarding health services that few studies can lay claim to being systemic. Almost without exception, reported research has dealt only partially with the consumer's decision process in selecting, and action process in utilizing, one or more sources of health care.

Discussing work on general demand for medical services, Feldstein notes that "multivariate studies have been few and have differed widely with regard to the variables, ... method, ... components of care studied."[185] Consequently, little is actually known about the net effects of particular variables. Considerably less research has been done on consumer demand for mental health services: goods about which there is possibly less popular understanding and more complex consumer behavior.

Studies which have dealt with the distribution of demand and the responses of various client groups to alternative sources of supply have been primarily concerned with the effects of physical accessibility. Only relatively recently have studies appeared which use some form of demand function for analyzing the interaction patterns between consumers and medical institutions.[186]

---

[j]Ro hastens to point out that other variables such as employment status and living arrangements also contribute to the length of hospital stay.[179]

Work done for the Chicago Regional Hospital Study includes some of the most systematic analysis of variation in supply and partially disaggregated analysis of consumer response to supply. Data reduction and regression techniques were used to develop several multivariate models for treating patient flows from communities to hospitals. These models were informed by theory and gave respectable predictive performances when tested with a sample drawn from patient data.[187]

Omission of several theoretically important variables, including race and mode of payment as well as physician referral, led to formulation of a second generation of simulation models which predict the movements of several consumer groups to hospitals.[188] This latter group of models is reported to have replicated use of the system moderately well, and has facilitated evaluating the locational efficiency of parts of the current medical care delivery system from the perspective of the consumers.[189]

As evidenced by the frequency with which the findings have been cited in the preceeding pages, the Chicago study has greatly advanced the theoretical and methodological base of health-services research. Yet, as Morrill and Earickson point out, patient perception and behavior are still inadequately understood, and current models still fail to accommodate adequately a number of variables which appear to exercise substantial influence on the ways in which health services are used.[190]

In the next chapter, we will specifically discuss mental health and mental health services. After defining types of mental illness, we will briefly treat the development of current programs for providing therapeutic care within the community in which clients reside.

3

Community Mental Health Services

Mental Health and Illness

To understand the purposes and tactics of community-based outpatient mental health services requires some understanding of what constitutes a mental disability, what some of the causes of these conditions are, and some forms or types of mental illness. Definitions of mental health and illness are marked by their lack of precision and prove to be the subjects of substantial disagreement in the psychiatric literature.[1] This in large part is a result of persisting lack of clear understanding concerning the causes of most conditions identified as mental illness.

Some Definitions

Both mental health and illness are commonly difined by symptoms or behavioral traits. Positive mental health suggests that an individual has a realistic or nondistortive orientation toward his social and physical environment, that he has (and is able to exercise) social skills in interpersonal relations, that his emotional life is personally satisfying, and that he meets reasonable role expectations of others who know him as, for example, fellow workers or members of a family. This definition depends heavily on the social context of the individual when, as Fromm points out, the society may be pathological and the deviant individual healthy.[2]

Jahoda identifies several characteristics of an emotionally healthy individual which are less dependent on the individual's social environment. These include an ability to cope with one's life situation, acceptance of self, sensitivity to social relations, a unifying outlook on life, and self-actualization. Neither of these approximations of what constitutes positive mental health serve as unambiguous guides to developing criteria for determining a state of health.[3]

Mental illness may be defined as the occurrence of psychological or neurological conditions giving rise to "gross deviation from a designated range of desirable behavioral variability."[4] Such a definition based as it is on symptoms such as nonconforming or maladaptive behavior, poses the ethical problem of who is to set the norms or criteria.[5]

Several symptomatic definitions commonly exist within a community; various lay definitions are instrumental in determining when a disturbed person should be encouraged to seek therapy, and professional definitions come to play in admission and prescription of therapy.[6] An individual's problem is seldom initially recognized as mental illness by friends and family.[7] Help is usually sought only after behavior becomes actively dysfunctional and extreme, or the individual's suffering becomes unmanagable.

Causes of Mental Illness

There are several widely acknowledged models or conceptions of the causes of mental illness, and widely differing opinion concerning their application. The disease concept holds that a disability is the result of genetic and biological factors. Mechanic points out that somatic causes have not been successfully identified for most psychiatric problems, and that attribution of a condition to a disease implies that the problem is within the individual rather than being in part a function of the social situation.[8]

A second model views psychopathology as a result of personality disturbances; that patterns of functioning developed from past experiences are the basis of an individual's current problems. Psychodynamic psychiatry is concerned primarily with the personality and undertakes to help the patient explore and come to understand the origins of the patient's personality. Recently, psychodynamic psychiatrists have come to accept one's social environment as playing a major role in mental illness.

A final conception identifies psychiatric distress as the result of the individual's environmental conditions rather than being physical or psychological disorders. Recognized difficulties are seen as problems of living, or the incongruence of a person's values and lifestyle and those widely held by others in the social setting.[9] When taken as a complete explanation of mental illness, this model fails to account for the fact that some people successfully adapt to a given environmental context or set of stresses while others do not.

These three models of the causation of mental illness represent the range of psychiatric views. Usually the conception held by a mental health professional emphasizes one of the three but includes elements of the other two. The current state of psychiatric knowledge precludes evaluating the relative validity of these points of view and encourages an eclectic approach both in interpreting causes and in designing therapeutic responses.[10]

Diagnostic Classes of Mental Illness[11]

Psychopathologies are classified by signs, or clinically observed indications of disease, and by symptoms, or the complaint of the patient. The resulting classification appears to differentiate kinds of illness rather than a scale of mental illness based on severity or resulting disability.[12]

The American Psychiatric Assocation differentiates three major types of conditions.[13] The first of these involves physical or chemical impairments of brain tissue, often called organic psychoses. Brain damage may result from trauma, metabolic imbalance, infection, or intoxication from drugs or industrial poisons. Several of these conditions may have symptoms similar to other forms of mental illness, and consequently complicate diagnosis. For example, epileptic psychoses may be manifest by hallucinations and other distortions in a manner similar to those connected with schizophrenia. In many cases, organic causes can be treated once the condition is properly identified. Treatment of chronic conditions, especially degenerative processes such as the onset of senility or the result of long-term addiction, is often limited to relieving the symptoms.

A second major classification is mental retardation or deficiency. Special education and counseling, at institutions for the retarded when the condition is severe, are forms of therapy calculated to help the individual realize his potential for self-support and a normal life. Treatment of mental deficiency differs enough both in nature and institutional arrangements from that for other mental disabilities that it is not investigated further in this report.

The third major diagnostic category, and the one with which we are primarily concerned in this investigation, is essentially the residuum of psychiatric conditions. Excluding problems stemming from structural changes in the brain, it consists of a broad set of disabilities for which there is no direct clinical identification of cause. This category encompasses a range of conditions varying in severity from psychoses, the most serious of the psychological illnesses, to psychoneuroses, which can cause individuals substantial discomfort but are usually comparatively minor.

We have adopted the APA schema for further subdividing this group of conditions into five classes: (1) psychotic, (2) psychoneurotic, (3) personality disorders, (4) drug or alcohol addiction or dependency, and (5) transient situational disturbances and adjustment reactions. Though these classes are based on symptoms or a reaction pattern identified with a condition, diagnoses on this basis often vary considerably among mental health professionals.

Psychoses are among the most serious mental illnesses, involving the emergence of dramatically new symptoms such as bizarre behavior and, commonly, disordered brain functions including acutely distorted perception and deranged thought processes. Major functional psychoses are schizophrenia and manic-depression.

Schizophrenia often affects young people and tends to progress through time. Most schizophrenia patients may be treated and released from hospitalization, but the minority who can not accumulate and often consitute about 50 percent of the hospital population. Manic-depressive reactions occur most commonly among middle-aged individuals. The course of this condition tends to be episodic and recurrent, but patients are usually returned to normal life.

Psychoneuroses are disturbances in the functioning of the personality, and show wide variation in their acuteness. The chief symptom of this group of problems is extreme or disabilitating anxiety. Forms of neurosis include anxiety reactions in which the anxiety is diffuse, hysterical conversion reactions in which the anxiety gives rise to an organic dysfunction such as paralysis or amnesia, and phobic states, in which the anxiety takes the form of a fear of a particular context, thing, or idea.

Personality disorders are continuing traits causing the individual to seek oblivion or cause trouble. Persons with this condition who are persistently antisocial are called psychopaths.

Addictions usually involve some ill-defined biochemical or metabolic change in the individual. The psychiatrist's concern in these cases is to examine for an underlying psychiatric condition, but in the absence of this patients primarily receive medical treatment.

Finally, transient situational disturbances may be very similar to anxiety reactions, but most commonly are dysfunctional responses to trauma brought about by childbirth, divorce, or other exceptionally stressful situations. Therapy in these cases is usually supportive and has as a purpose teaching the individual to cope with stress.

Some Characteristics of Therapeutic Intervention

A general theoretical definition of psychiatric care is difficult. The care or service is usually a complex package consisting of several components or types of treatments. In the case of outpatient services, the major topic of concern here, treatment may consist of individual analytic psychotherapy in some form or a less long-range form of directive or organic treatment, it may involve group therapy, and it may be combined with partial hospitalization. Differing goals for treatment may suggest the combination which a therapist prescribes, as may the presented problems of the client, and the financial and apparent cognitive resources of the client.

The complex nature of outpatient mental health care, and of factors influencing the selection of components to be combined as a proposed package of treatments for a client, complicate efforts to analyze differences in quality of care. Similar combinations of treatments for clients with similar complaints will still vary in effectiveness in a manner which at least partially precludes qualitative evaluation. Additionally, differences in expenditures among clients for ostensibly the same services may primarily represent purchases of different amenities which have an unknown impact on the effectiveness of the treatment. For example, office visits to a private psychiatrist may be differentiated from individual therapy at a clinic only by the privacy and other physical amenities of the setting.

Outpatient mental health care is seldom an end in itself, but rather is sought as a means to obtaining a more positive state of mental health. Thus, in addition to being a complex good, therapy is also an intermediate good. While the etiology or causes of mental illness are only partly known, it appears that one source is stress stemming, for example, from living conditions or social relationships, and that even nutrition bears on the mental health of an individual. Resources allocated to decreasing stress or to improving the individual's ability to solve problems or cope with stress are consequently alternatives or perhaps complements to therapy as means of obtaining positive mental health.

Mental health care may be defined as a service which aids in managing or reversing undesired mental conditions which are actual or potential.[14] This definition includes both removing or controlling existing disability and preventive action to avoid the occurrence of disability. While we shall be concerned in this study primarily with ways of providing outpatient care for the mentally ill in a manner which will encourage its effective use, we will also discuss some services which are tactically important for prevention.

This definition of mental health care also suggests that the therapy may involve several different services. Various treatments or components of care may be complementary, that is, may be combined to provide the desired therapy. Alternatively, some combinations of components may be substituted for others, for example, partial or full hospitalization for outpatient services. Explanations of variations in use of various components must take into account the use of other services, especially where substitutions may occur.[a] Similarly, demand for various formal mental health services may be affected by consumer substitution of informal services such as advice from friends or clergymen, or membership in voluntary groups such as churches or ethnic organizations which serve some of the functions of therapeutic intervention.

Therapeutic Approaches

Several forms of psychotherapy are currently used in outpatient treatment of mental illness. Perhaps the most famous of these is Freudian psychoanalysis, which emphasizes the role of an individual's early experiences in current problems. Therapy usually involves several sessions a week, at which the patient is encouraged to recall dreams and to try to make conscious that which is unconscious. Somewhat differently, psychoanalytically based psychotherapy deals with current and past thoughts and experiences, and has the purpose of resolving recognized problems through understanding their origins. This form of psychotherapy may involve some direction from the therapist and is less intensive than analysis, usually involving one interview session a week.

---

[a]A major criticism of several of the studies discussed in Chapter 2 involved oversight of this characteristic of the health delivery system.

Supportive psychotherapy primarily concentrates on resolving immediate problems, placing less emphasis on understanding the background or origins of the problems. This form of therapy is commonly eclectic concerning theory and tends to recognize a substantial social or interpersonal element in problems of mental health. Therapeutic sessions may be once a week and involve explicit interpretation and considerable direction by the therapist. Supportive therapy can often be provided effectively by individuals with less professional mental health training than psychiatrists or psychologists such as by social workers, nurses, or clergymen.

A recent form of treatment is behavior therapy, which seeks to resolve the patient's problems by changing habits or attitudes which appear to be the source of trouble. This approach has been used most successfully in dealing with neuroses such as phobias and anxiety responses, but may be more widely applicable. Techniques range from role-playing to operant conditioning in which desired behavior is rewarded and undesirable is punished, for example by a mild shock. Attractive features of behavior therapy include the possibility of securing some desired results in a short time and less dependence on communication, especially verbalization by the patient, than the first three modes of therapy require.

A fifth form of treatment is group therapy, which may use theory and methods from several of the other approaches mentioned, but deals with more than one patient at a time. Since many presented problems involve interpersonal relations in a marriage or family, group therapy is a logical and sometimes the only effective means of intervention. Therapeutic groups of eight to ten people, meeting with a therapist, offer some economies in treatment while they do not serve precisely the same purpose as individual therapy. A group may be led by a therapeutic team, and therapists may include professionals and also paraprofessionals who have received some training in psychiatric care. By extension, some sensitivity and encounter groups may be viewed as forms of group therapy.

A sixth form of treatment is the use of psychoactive drugs. Tranquilizers and antidepressants are usually used to control or modify the disturbance, so that people may make more effective use of group or individual therapy and may remain in their communities during treatment. Drug treatment may also be a major part of therapy in transient situations; cases in which anxiety in response to stresses may be resolved by obtaining a period of rest or relaxation.

The latter four forms of treatment, often in combination, tend to be short-term relative to analysis and analytical psychotherapy. Clearly the preferred combination of treatments depends on a number of factors such as the condition and attitudes of the client and the purposes of therapy. While most clients prefer individual therapy, and many desire the more thorough approach of analysis or analytic therapy, shortages of money and manpower make short-term forms of therapy attractive as the therapeutic components of a public mental health program.

Some Exceptional Features of Demand for Mental Health Services

Utilization of mental health care and demand for components of the service differ from consumption of most market goods and services which the consumer directly chooses on the basis of available information. The client of mental health services expresses a demand for therapy or care with some preference expressed for the type of treatment or the nature of the service desired. This demand is then translated by the therapist into a treatment package or combination of components.[b] Thus the demand for kinds of treatment, their frequency, and even their quality is properly considered as derived demand or the response of the therapist to the initial demand for mental health care. The therapist thus acts in the dual role of broker or consumer advisor and as a supplier of the service.

The derived nature of demand for mental health services is significant in its impact on consumer choice in utilizing a service and in understanding the process by which decisions are made concerning components of the service which will be consumed. The consumer's choice is largely limited to seeking care, although substitutions may be made among suppliers offering differing packages of treatment and other service features such as location and price.[17] The consumer ususlly may also veto the choices made by the therapist by rejecting the prescribed treatment.[18]

The therapist's role in prescribing the treatments, constituting the therapy which the consumer receives, defines the second portion of a two-stage decision process.[19] Thus, while the consumer exercises choice in seeking care, this choice is limited by the control over access to treatment exercised by the therapist.

Within the range of choice delimited by the role and behavior of the therapist, the consumer's choice is further dependent on available information and the ability to use it. While traditional demand analysis assumes extensive availability of information, a number of studies point up the extent of consumer ignorance in purchasing behavior concerning relatively simple market goods.[20] These studies also reveal the tendency for higher income persons to be better informed and to be better able to use this information than are lower income individuals.

In the case of mental health services—a highly complex good—knowledge informing choice refers both to the available sources of care and their attributes

---

[b]Investigation of psychiatric practice suggests that class differences are reflected in prescribed treatment programs, with lower-class patients receiving more custodial care and less analytic psychotherapy than do middle- and upper-class patients.[15] F.C. Redlich found that the high prevalence of schizophrenics in treatment coming from the lower classes could be accounted for by the differences in treatment and opportunity for rehabilitation which they received.[16]

and to information supporting assessment of need for mental health services and of benefits to be derived from consuming various of these services.[c] Discussing consumer ignorance as a major market imperfection affecting consumption of mental health care, Sloan assesses the inability of consumers to effectively evaluate the services received, to choose among alternative suppliers, and to effectively use preventive services.[21] He sees consumer ignorance as primarily a function of poor information.

In addition to availability of information, ability to use information is yet another constraint on consumer choice. Education appears to be a major determinant of an individual's ability to apply information in selecting an effective course of action, as well as to gain access to information.[22] This differential ability gives higher income persons a comparative advantage as consumers of mental health care. Similarly, valuation of alternative opportunities and benefits appear to vary among groups of the population, based on attitudes concerning, for example, mental health and public service agencies. Finally, psychiatric disability can be expected to affect the individual's competence to behave as a rational consumer in seeking and using information. While this may frequently be the case with people who are acutely disabled to the extent that they require hospitalization, it would appear that this is substantially less likely among people seeking outpatient services.[23]

As a final issue in this brief discussion of some of the features of demand for mental health services which differentiates its use from that of other commodities, mention should be made of the extent to which demand for psychiatric care is descretionary.

A major concern of this study is the discrepancy between need and demand for mental health services. Need may be psychiatrically defined as the mental health care required by a person based on the individual's condition. In contrast, demand is the desire for mental health care, usually measured in terms of actual consumption of services. It appears safe to assume that a substantial proportion of the psychiatrically disabled in the population are not consumers of mental health services in a manner commensurate with their need. Further, it appears that such individuals are disproportionately lower-income people. While there is wide agreement on these points,[24] empirical verification must await careful epidemiological surveys revealing the distribution of incidence among various segments of the population.

Aggregate demand in terms of use is commonly employed as the basis for providing new service capacity. Such an approach is unresponsive to latent demand, especially in the form of need which remains unrevealed because of lack of consumer information, unacceptability of the current supply of mental health services, or some combination of these and other factors. Where

---

[c]This suggests the desirability of a public information program as a tactic for changing the proportionate distribution of use.

expressed desire for service exceeds the need of an individual, it is reasoned that the therapist can appropriately control the amount of the service provided.

A variant on the definition of need given above is that of nondiscretionary demand for a good. In other words, a good may be a need if it is required for basic human functioning and there are no effective substitutes for it. Tiebout and Houston identify such goods as "necessity goods," and give as illustrations food and shelter.[25]

Psychiatric care may most appropriately be considered a need in cases of acute mental illness, where functioning is drastically impaired. In these cases, it is a nondiscretionary good if the condition is to be relieved. The consumer's income and the price and other characteristics of the service would tend to have limited or no impact on the amount of service consumed. In some extreme cases, persons are legally required to undertake psychiatric treatment.

Individuals with less extreme impairments have more discretion in consuming mental health care. In these cases, the person's desire or want for the service becomes a major factor in consumption. Some substitutes for psychiatric care and choices among suppliers of psychiatric services become options for the consumer. This appears to be the case for most clients of outpatient mental health services.

Where discretion among consumers for a service, passing judgment in differentiating between clients for whom the good is a need and those for whom it is a want becomes ethically troublesome. Increasingly, the notion of need is being expanded to include consumption of necessity goods adequate to support higher levels of human functioning. Additionally, the public has come to accept equal access to mental health care as a human right. These and other arguments developed in Chapter 4, underlay public support, at least in principle, for providing subsidized mental health services.

The Magnitude and Distribution of Mental Illness

The importance of mental illness as a social problem can be partially assessed by considering the magnitude and distribution of psychiatric disability in the population. Epidemiological studies would supply this information, but there are no national studies of this sort[d] and the several carried out in select cities over the last two decades show dramatic variability in their findings.[e]

---

[d]While no actual counts are available, the estimated prevalence of disabling mental and nervous conditions among persons from families with incomes of $7,000 or more is 4.2 per 1000, and for people with family incomes of $2,000 or less, the estimated rate is 26.4 per 1000, or greater than six times the rate for the higher income group.[27]

[e]No epidemiological data on the actual incidence of mental illness is available for San Francisco, or for the population of the Westside catchment area, which is the area used as a case study in the second half of this study.

The Midtown Manhattan Study, the most widely known example of recent epidemiological research, concluded that about one-quarter of those surveyed were sufficiently emotionally disabled as to require therapy, and only 18.5 percent were considered mentally healthy.[26] This study also found that mental health was positively related to socioeconomic status,[f] as was use of pyschiatric services by those who were impaired.[g]

A similar study, based on data for fifteen years, was done of a rural county in Canada.[30] Findings on the frequency and distribution of mental illness were comparable to the midtown study, and neurosis was found to be most prevalent among members of the lower class.

Not only would it be inappropriate to generalize from these community studies, but additional studies using other methods have found very different rates of prevalence. Two reviews of a number of reports on epidemiological research show that identified prevalence varies from 1 to 60 percent of the population.[31] It appears that a widely quoted estimate that 10 percent of the noninstitutionalized population living in urban areas suffer from identifiable psychological disorders is a conservative figure.[32]

Several statistics concerning the use of mental health services further aid in understanding the magnitude of mental illness as a social issue. One recent estimate places the number of American people seeking mental health service, inpatient and outpatient from all sources, at three million a year.[33] About 37 percent of all hospital beds in this country are occupied by the mentally ill.[34] In terms of cost of service, nearly three billion dollars were spent on care and treatment at all mental hospitals in 1969.[35]

A study of the mentally ill entering therapy in New Haven gives additional information on the distribution of care among social groups.[36] Classifying a six-month sample of first admissions by five social groupings, Hollingshead and Redlich found the highest rates of hospitalization and the longest duration of hospitalization among the lowest social stratum. On the other hand, the highest rate of use of public and private outpatient therapy was among the upper social strata. A major conclusion of this study was that social group membership was a significant predictor of the way in which people entered therapy, the kind of therapy that they got, and the duration of their therapy.[37]

The distributional topic receiving the most research attention is the relationship between social class and hospitalization for psychotic conditions. Several studies, often using less than 100 observations, found an inverse relationship between admissions to hospitalization and social class, with the

[f] A second report on the Midtown Manhattan Study found that while neuroses were proportionately most prevalent among people from higher-status groups, stress led to a disproportionately high rate of psychosis among lower-status groups.[28]

[g] 12.5 percent of the highest socioeconomic group were identified as impaired and 20 percent of these were receiving treatment, while 47.3 percent of the lowest group were classed as impaired and 1 percent of these were receiving treatment.[29]

lowest class accounting for twice the rate of any other socioeconomic group.[38] Studies using larger samples have additionally found a continuous inverse relationship between class level and incidence of hospitalization, with a greater difference in rate of admission between the lowest and second lowest classes than between any other two groups.[39]

While this evidence cannot be used to predict incidence of mental illness by social grouping, it does suggest a distributional issue and provides a framework for briefly discussing several explanations found in the literature. The first of these explanations is etiological; that lower-class persons suffer from blocked aspirations and from social and economic insecurity,[40] or that deprivation and frustration resulting from membership in a low socioeconomic group give greater rise to mental illness than found among other groups.[41] Two related explanations deal with social-class membership resulting from mental ill health or deviant behavior. The first of these deals with the downward intergenerational mobility of people exceptionally susceptible to mental illness, and is in part an effort to explain the concentration of schizophrenia in the lowest class and status positions.[42] The second of these explanations is intragenerational; that a person with mental illness problems "drifts" downward occupationally, in income, and in cost of housing.[43] Some studies have attempted to investigate this by checking on the occupational status of their patient sample for a several year period prior to hospitalization.[44]

A final explanation of differential rates of hospitalization is that social reaction to mental illness and tolerance of deviant behavior varies among social groups.[45] Thus poorer families would be less able to care for and support mentally disabled persons, psychiatrists more readily prescribe hospitalization for individuals from lower socioeconomic groups,[46] and societal acceptance of deviant behavior decreases with decreasing social class membership.

Clearly, mental illness constitutes a significant social problem. About one-fifth of the population is disturbed enough to benefit from therapy, and one-tenth is psychiatrically disabled. Even though a small fraction of people in each of these groups currently receive therapy, expenditures for mental health services are substantial. Finally, the distribution of mental illness appears to disproportionately affect those who are least able to pay for psychiatric care. We now turn to a discussion of community-based mental health services which have been developed in response to the social implications of mental illness.

The Treatment of Mental Illness in the United States

Care for the mentally and emotionally ill was, until nearly the twentieth century, predominately left to the family. Public concern and some expression of responsibility did, however, begin to emerge in America during the colonial period. Benjamin Franklin is identified with a campaign which succeeded in gaining admission of the mentally ill to Philadelphia's Pennsylvania Hospital in 1756. The first hospital for the mentally ill was opened in Williamsburg, Virginia in 1773.[47]

Dr. Benjamin Rush, working at Pennsylvania Hospital in the late 1700s, was the first American to deal scientifically with mental illness. While his teaching, research, and practice influenced many doctors and others in the United States, public treatment of the mentally ill primarily consisted of holding them in jails or the few asylums that were available.

It was in response to this inhumane and counter therapeutic treatment that Dorothea Lynde Dix crusaded for public awareness and responsibility for the mentally ill, and for the establishment of mental hospitals. While her work resulted in the construction of a number of mental hospitals during the mid-nineteenth century, admissions and transfers from jails soon led to extreme overcrowding.[48]

The late 1800s was a period of considerable scientific inquiry into the causes and cures of mental illness. Physiological and psychological origins were investigated, with Sigmund Freud's later development of psychoanalysis focusing professional interest on psychogenetic or nonphysical causes of pathology.

Legislation in 1890 made New York the first state to assume responsibility for institutional treatment of the psychopathological. Other states followed with legislation and hospital construction; however, Clifford Beers exposed the conditions and treatment of inmates in these institutions as ethically reprehensible. Beer's efforts for reform led to the organization of the National Committee for Mental Hygiene. This group emphasized means for preventing mental illness and public education concerning mental illness and therapy.

The large numbers of draft rejections on psychiatric grounds and the emotional problems of many service men returning from World War II brought widespread public concern over the magnitude and costs of the mental health problem in the United States.[h] One result was the National Mental Health Act of 1946, which provided federal funding for mental health services, research and training, and enabled the National Institute of Mental Health to be established in 1949.

During the 1950s, outpatient clinics were established in a large number of cities, and psychiatric care began to become a service commonly provided by general hospitals located in urban areas. New psychiatric drugs made it possible to maintain and treat many patients on a part-time basis in their communities, in contrast to the earlier tendency to require long-term total hospitalization. Several states, led by New York in 1954, passed community mental health service acts, providing partial state funding for locally administered psychiatric care programs.[49]

---

[h]Approximately 1.75 million men had been rejected on grounds of mental or emotional disturbances.[51] Over 380,000 personnel were discharged from the service because of psychiatric disability during World War II.[52]

Mental Health was now a subject of popular concern, but contemporary mobilization of support for extensive public provision of therapeutic care for the mentally disturbed stemmed from the 1961 publication of *Action for Mental Health*.[50] This programmatic report was the product of a five-year study by representatives from thirty-six organizations, acting as the congressionally established Joint Commission on Mental Illness and Health. Recommendations by the commission included expansion of services both in scope and availability, reducing the size of state hospitals, and locating many mental health services in the residential community of the patients.

These recommendations prompted President Kennedy's 1963 Message to Congress, calling for "a new type of health facility"—the community mental health center. This first presidential message to Congress in behalf of mental health services led to passage of the Mental Retardation Facilities and Community Mental Health Centers Construction Act of 1963. This legislation authorized $150 million in federal matching funds over a three-year period to states for construction of new or expanded community mental health facilities. The money, distributed among the states on the basis of population, could cover up to two-thirds of construction costs.[53] Additional legislation passed in 1965 extended federal assistance to local mental health care by establishing a staffing grant program which would pay a portion of the personnel costs for new or expanded service programs for a period of up to fifty-one months.[54]

Administrative regulations, required by the 1963 act, specified the services which a community mental health center must provide to qualify for federal assistance. The five "essential elements" of a community program include outpatient services, inpatient services, partial hospitalization including at least day care, 24-hour emergency services at some agency location, and consultation and educational services to local service agencies and related professionals. Since this represents the minumum level of performance acceptable to the federal government, this listing of services has become the basic definition of a community mental health program.

These regulations also specified five services which, when provided in addition to the five essential services, constitute an "adequate" community mental health program. These additional services include diagnosis, rehabilitation, precare and aftercare including half-way houses, and research and training.

The term *community mental health center* has caused some confusion. The component services do not need to be offered at a single location, but the federal program does require that they be coordinated within a community, that a client eligible for one service may be transferred to other services within the program, and that community programs be components of larger mental health service plans for a city and state. The term "community" refers to a catchment area or a service district with a resident population of between 75,000 and 200,000 people.

A major purpose of this influential legislation was to decentralize the provision of mental health care, locating it in a manner which is conveniently accessible to the homes of clients and their families, and to encourage the programs to be accountable to the population served. While delimiting the size of populations to be served was a major step toward decentralization, it appears that the notion of a catchment area has led many professionals to think of these populations as relatively homogeneous and of the areas as entities in a sociological sense. As we will see in the case study which follows, an urban subpopulation of this size commonly contains several social groups, each with attitudes and values which differentially affect their use of community mental health services.

This brief developmental history of mental health care in the United States points up the increasing public assumption of responsibility for providing professional services. By replacing family responsibility for the psychiatrically disabled, institutional care became increasingly centralized, and, partly as a function of being remotely located, became primarily custodial. Over the last two decades, new drugs and increasing public awareness of the nature and consequences of mental illness opened the way for a community-oriented reorganization of mental health services, culminating in the 1963 federal legislation supporting localized provision of psychiatric care.

This federal policy and funding prompted a radical change in the approach and method of providing mental health services. The emphasis of public programs was changed to prevention and to early detection and treatment. Services began to become widely available and located accessibly within urban areas. Finally, as Mechanic points out, this legislation "implicitly endorsed the viewpoint that mental illness is not inherently different from the larger range of psychological difficulties common in the community."[55]

4

Welfare Considerations in the Use of Mental Health Services

As discussed in the preceeding chapter, provision of mental health services has become an increasingly accepted function of the local, state, and federal governments. Welfare economics provides an analytical framework and a source of general principles for guiding both the design and the provision of services such as community mental health care.

Principles relating to how the service should be supplied include the desirability of making alterations in a program which result in Pareto optimal changes where this is possible, and concern with the distribution effects of alternative program designs. Welfare economics also provides rationales for public involvement in provision of a good when conditions for the market acting as an effective allocative device are not operating. Immediately apparent reasons for market failure include the existence of a monopoly, inadequate consumer information, and technological spillovers in production or consumption. Public intervention is especially desirable in the cases of collective consumption and merit goods. In the following pages, we analyze the characteristics of community mental health services and their use, which suggest whether they are most appropriately provided by the public or the private sectors.

Mental Health Care as an Individual and Collective Consumption Service

Mental health services have characteristics which make them similar to other goods and services which are only supplied by the private market, but they also have characteristics which differentiate them from these other goods. Goods commonly sold by firms and purchased by individuals are often referred to as "individual-consumption goods," because the consumer enjoys all of the benefit or utility to be derived from the good and usually pays a price which covers the full cost of production and marketing.

Outpatient mental health care is an individual-consumption service in the sense that the client may be excluded from receiving therapy unless an assessed price is paid. Other means of exclusion such as an admissions policy or discriminatory intake procedures are possible as well. Mental health care is also similar to services usually provided by the private sector in that consumption by an individual precludes another person receiving service from the particular therapist at that point in time. In other words, the individual consumer makes exclusive use of the resources employed in providing therapeutic service to him.

45

However, outpatient mental health care is also a "collective-consumption service," in the sense that there are benefits and costs from an individual's consumption behavior which affect other parties.[1] These extraconsumer effects are often called spillovers or externalities.

To the extent that the benefits of consuming mental health services are not fully realized by the direct consumer, that is, the person who must pay the price for the service in the private sector, people will tend to consume less of the service than is socially desirable because the value to indirect beneficiaries will not be fully considered.[2] Existence of extraconsumer effects is a major rationale for social or public-sector support through subsidy or regulation for the purpose of encouraging consumption of the particular service in a manner which will result in greater total benefit to all members of the public.

Emphasizing ways in which outpatient mental health care is a collective-consumption service, the following discussion treats three major features of this service. These include various ways in which consumption is interdependent or involves externalities as briefly discussed above, the role of uncertainty in incidence of demand and effectiveness of treatment, and the merit good or social valuation of the service, which may for various reasons differ from the benefit which a prospective client recognizes. While characteristics of mental health care of the first two types are found to be important, the merit good arguments strongly suggest the desirability of public intervention in the supply of this service.

Consumer Interdependence

An externality or spillover may be defined as an "unpriced effect";[3] the interdependence of an individual's profit or utility on another party's production or consumption.[4] Thus consumer interdependence may result in a benefit received from someone else's behavior without charge, or a cost incurred without compensation. Outpatient mental health services appear to be affected, in varying degrees, by three types of consumer interdependence: direct, indirect, and spatial extraconsumer effects.

Direct Consumer Interdependence

Direct consumer interdependence results when the behavior of one person effects the utility of another individual. In general terms, an external effect of consumption is present when:

$$U^A = U^A (X_1, X_2, \ldots, X_m, Y_1)$$

where $X_i = A$'s activities

$Y_i = B$'s activities

Applying this to the case of mental health services, the utility of A may depend on an activity Y_1 of B such as consumption of preventive or therapeutic care. When the marginal external effect of B's consumption dU^A/dY_1 is greater than zero, A realizes a benefit without necessarily paying for it. An external effect is "Pareto-relevant" when the extent of B's activity can be modified such that the externally affected party A can be made better off without the acting party B being made worse off, that is, where there is a gain from trade.[5]

A classic example of direct consumer interdependence in the health literature is communicable disease, in which immunization or timely treatment of B would decrease the probability of A contracting the disease.[a] In such a situation, both parties would be better off if A could compensate B to consume more of the service. An exchange of this sort in the private sector would require a payment method, which would in turn require that those who are to be compensated be identifiable and few enough to make compensation practicable.[7] Where the external benefits generated by a consumer's behavior cannot be appropriated or handled through some compensation mechanism, private consumption of the service to produce the desired state will not be at a level which will result in the greatest net benefit to all of the affected parties. Continued existence of externalities in consumption also commonly leads to underproduction from a social perspective, since demand is affected.[b] Such a set of conditions suggests the desirability of governmental intervention in the form of subsidy in providing the service or regulation of behavior.

Mental illness is not considered communicable. Thus the production of

---

[a]The extreme case of consumer interdependence is the "pure public good," defined by Samuelson as one which is available to all, whether or not the consumer pays. The "collective consumption" nature of these goods means that each unit of the good provided is consumed simultaneously by each and every individual, without diminishing the good available for consumption by others. Common examples include national defense, broadcast information, and basic research.[6] Using this definition, therapy consumed by individuals is not a collective consumption good; however, a prevention program consisting of public information on mental hygiene and of action to improve stress-inducing conditions giving rise to mental illness or its emergence could be considered as collective or indivisible among the residents of a locality where such services are provided.

[b]Ambiguous signals concerning demand and consumer valuation can lead to underproduction in the Pareto optimum sense, whether that service is provided by the private or the public sector. Samuelson, among others, points out that institutional choice of levels of providing public goods is among a set of *feasible* institutional arrangements and is seldom made entirely on the basis of the economically desirable Pareto optimum. That is, factors other than economic are relevant and important to institutional considerations, with the consequence that the constrained set of feasible alternative supply positions does not have to satisfy the necessary conditions of Pareto optimality.[9]

mental health through consumption of appropriate services does not appear to have the direct consumer interdependence of the type just discussed. Acute mental illness in a family is often an indicator of high risk of mental illness for other members of the family, and it is sometimes suggested that the pathologies of an individual affect the mental health of others in the living unit, but causality has not been established.[8]

In terms of costs, however, congestion of an agency supplying therapy can be a direct external effect of consuming mental health services. This may operate when, for example, an increase in the number of patients seeking care lowers the value of the service to all consumers. While congestion is commonly taken to mean a situation in which demand for a service exceeds the capacity of the supplier to produce that service, the congestion effect may also result from lower levels of demand.[10] As discussed in Chapter 2, this problem has been recognized in some of the research dealing with hospital utilization.

Indirect Consumer Interdependence

While utilization of mental health services appears to result in few direct external effects, several consumer interdependencies do appear in the second round impacts of mental health condition or consumption of the service. Identification of these external effects requires analyzing the consequences of the service or viewing consumption of the service as generating an intermediate good. Thus disability and antisocial acts stemming from mental illness may be defined as unmet need or underconsumption of the service. Consequences and spillovers of individual psychiatric or emotional disability include such social costs as:

1. Difficulty in securing employment, resulting in demand for unemployment compensation and other direct public support[11]
2. Deviant behavior and disruption of others, increasing demand for other social care-taking and public safety services, hence expenditures[c]
3. Lower productivity leading to higher production costs, as well as lower levels of contribution by the individual to the community and to the public fisc[d]

---

[c]A study of social costs of retaining schizophrenic patients in the community lists twenty-two problems stemming from the burdensome behavior of the patients. These problems varied from total disruption of the family and the ability for others in the family to continue jobs or schooling, to odd speech and ideas.[12] Mechanic speaks of the fact that mental illness is frequently socially disruptive in that it may frighten or threaten others and that it involves a large element of social unpredictability.[13]

[d]To the extent that publically provided mental health services enhance human capacity and that this bears on productivity, this may be interpreted as a pecuniary external economy affecting local firms; an "urbanization economy" of agglomeration in Hoover's terms.[14] Differences between the earning power of individuals receiving and not receiving treatment

4. Higher rates of family disorganization and problems with child care, leading to lower levels of aggregate public well-being and increased demand for remedial services[16]

These indirect or secondary consequences appear as interpersonal costs of not maintaining positive mental health status. Primarily because these extraconsumer effects are difficult to measure and to attribute to beneficiaries, they bolster the argument for public intervention in the provision of mental health services. Furthermore, most of the indirect effects of underconsuming mental health services involve public expenditures. Where the cost of mental health services is less than the cost of providing services which ameliorate the secondary effects of mental illness, subsidized provision of therapeutic care would be justified on the basis of economic efficiency.

Spatial External Effects

The physical distributions of external effects, especially spillovers which may cross jurisdictional boundaries, are important in budgeting and in governmental organization to provide sets of services. These externalities are widely treated by welfare economics, partly because they are among the easiest to observe.[17]

Programs which may be classified as human resource services such as education, local recreation, and mental health are not as widely acknowledged to have extensive spatial externalities. These are services which are often only available to citizens of the jurisdiction providing them. Failure to identify spatial externalities in these cases largely stems from a static view; when time is introduced, mobility of the consumers must be taken into account. Thus, to the extent that these services enhance the capacity of consumers to lead fuller and more productive lives and that mobility occurs involving taking these capacities (or incapacities) with them, these programs (or their failures) evidence important spatial extraconsumer effects.

An often cited example is the impact of poor educational programs, in a region where migrants grew up, on the social problems of cities to which these migrants have moved. Similarly, the mental health of migrants, as affected by their consumption of appropriate services in the communities from which they come, will have the character of a spatial externality when they move to another community. Consequently, service and related consumption deficiencies in the community of origin will contribute to social problems, based on untreated disabilities, in the destination community; will probably cause the resettlement process to be more disruptive personally; and will contribute disproportionately to demand for mental health services in the jurisdiction to which they move.

---

for similar presented problems is a commonly discussed measure of benefit for programs of this sort.[15]

High rates of interjurisdictional migration resulting in spatial extraconsumer effects pose problems in organizing both regional and interregional systems for providing mental health services, and constitute a major rationale for federal subsidy to local provision of these services.

The Role of Uncertainty

Several collective consumption features of mental health services have been identified. Apart from these, however, the nature of demand for therapeutic care has characteristics which make public intervention attractive. Risk and uncertainty are involved in consumption and provision for consumption of psychiatric services, first because of the irregular incidence of mental illness and consequent disability, and second because it is not known whether treatment will yield the desired results with no unexpected adverse side effects.

A widespread response to these situations is to insure against them; to collectively assume financial responsibility for possible incidence of demand.[18] Mental health care is increasingly included as a benefit in private health insurance policies. The desirability of "social" insurance or coinsurance is indicated if uncertainty is so great as to make solely private provision of insurance unprofitable. This has been, in part, the case with Medicare and similar programs covering particular subgroups of the population.

As yet, neither private nor public insurance covers all the uncertainty with respect to illness and treatment.[e] Complicating the provision of insurance as an efficient means to supporting or encouraging highly purposeful consumption is the issue of "moral hazard," or excessive consumption because the good is freely available to the individual.[20] There is a growing literature on medical insurance with respect to this point, but it appears to be inconclusive.

In addition to covering the unexpected costs of illness, Weisbrod points out that because of uncertainty, even the individual-consumption benefits of a commodity such as mental health services can have characteristics of a pure collective-consumption good.[21] This comes about for two reasons; infrequency and uncertainty of purchase of the particular good, and the difficulty of expanding or recommencing production of the good. Concerning the first reason, current production assures the availability of the service and thus positively enters into the utility functions of *prospective* users, satisfying an option demand and thus generating an external benefit. Potential availability of the service, as Margolis points out, does not create congestion, and to the extent that all can afford to acquire the service, its potential availability is a pure public good.[22]

---

[e] Arrow points out that ideal insurance would cover recovery rather than simply financing purchase of services in the event of illness.[19]

The second reason which Weisbrod discusses is essentially an inventory problem. Expansion or recommencement of production at the time the occasional purchasers wish to consume a good may be difficult or impossible. This assumes that the good can not be stored. This is the case with psychotherapeutic services since these involve direct personal interaction between the patient and clinician. Consequently, some excess capacity or supply in excess of current demand may be justified on the basis of fluctuations in demand. However, the cost of idle capacity must be balanced against the speed with which production can be expanded and the costs of delaying consumption when demand occurs, as with the case of waiting lists.

The uncertainty underlying both the frequency distribution of demand in time and space, and technical problems affecting the speed with which supply can and will respond to peaks in demand, suggest that information problems exist in the private market and that consequent supply by private enterprise may be less than that which is socially desired. In this case, the social welfare may be improved through public subsidy or provision of these services. Weisbrod suggests that the feasability of assessing user charges varies inversely with the extent to which these two conditions exist with respect to a commodity.[23]

Mental Health Care as a Merit Good

Consumer interdependence and the role of uncertainty in the use of mental health services provide substantial arguments for social involvement in the supply of these services. However, evaluation of psychiatric care as a "merit good" provides an especially strong set of arguments, based on welfare economics, for public-sector provision of these services. As the following discussion demonstrates, merit arguments depend on some of the demand and consumption characteristics discussed earlier, but they also supplement the case made in the preceeding pages for the appropriateness of governmental subsidy and controls.

Merit goods are essentially individual-consumption goods as defined earlier, but commodities which have become endowed with the public interest.[24] The public interest aspect becomes the source of externalities from consumption, making the merit case in effect a private-plus-public good.[25] Community mental health care, as with most publically provided urban services, is properly classified as a merit good.

Merit goods, by their public provision at zero or subsidized price, represent an interference with consumer sovereignty in that their supply is intended to induce more consumption of the specific good or service than would be the case if the individual had to budget and pay for its full cost. Because consumer sovereignty is a long-cherished element of this society's ideology and a basic mechanism in the market economy on which allocative economics depends, discussants of merit goods commonly show some uneasiness at this imposition. However, the major argument for merit goods identifies a market failure; that primarily because of imperfect information, persons would consume too little or too much of the good.

Head's classification of properties of merit goods provides a useful framework for analyzing mental health services in this context.[26] These properties include: preference-distortion problems, distributional problems, and public goods problems.

Preference-Distortion Problems

This category of problems deals with imperfect information and decision-making ability on the part of the prospective consumer. Preference-distortion takes a number of forms which require attention in public policy analysis. One such form is the difference in attitude toward the service after consumption from that held before consumption. Thus an individual may realize increased well-being from having consumed mental health care and evaluates the benefits as being acceptably greater than the costs, but this individual may have earlier resisted consuming the service because with the information available his evaluation was different.

Social stigma attached to mental illness and need for treatment continue to make the cost of seeking assistance very high for many people.[27] Similarly, information concerning when, where, and how to seek help is not widely available.[28] Patterns of treatment and their effectiveness are even less widely known and understood. These conditions suggest the value of more effective effort to increase public information and even to change public attitudes toward mental illness and its treatment. Public information programs technically may be interpreted as public goods, but their purpose in this case is to change consumer preferences. Public provision or partial subsidy of mental health service can further reduce the sum of the price and other costs faced by the individual in seeking to remedy his disability.

In addition to shortage of information, various socioeconomic groups appear to perceive mental illness and regard the value of treatment differently. Thus the blue-collar or lower-middle income people appear to view mental illness as a source of stigma and consequently tend to refuse to acknowledge it in themselves or their family. Lower income groups place a relatively low priority on securing mental health services since maintenance of physical health, resaonable diet, and shelter constitute more immediate problems. Inducing greater consumption of mental health services among such groups involves not only improving the supply of information, but carefully designing the way in which the service is supplied such that the expected benefits will adequately outweigh the costs incurred in consuming the good.[f] This suggests that the merit quality of the good, with reference to the preference-distortion problem, is affected by intergroup differences in perceiving the need and the value of the good as these affect consumption.

The problem of preferences leading to behavior that is in the individual's own best interests is further complicated when the disability directly affects the bases for making decisions and the processes of arriving at decisions to consume psychiatric care. When the individual's condition is so acute that his judgment diverges drastically from his self-interest, and where an alternative is well known to be better for him, public intervention may take the form of compelling him to undertake therapy. This is, of course, the extreme case and, when involuntary treatment is involved, constitutes interference not only with consumer sovereignty in the common sense but with individual freedom as a civil right as well.

Toward the other end of a disability range, the individual with minor symptoms may, perhaps for some of the reasons just cited, delay consuming treatment services. In many cases, it is thought that early detection and treatment of mental illness or emotional problems can arrest or reverse the condition.[30] This suggests that public provision and encouragement to use mental health services to overcome consumer resistance to early treatment will result in personal and public economies.[g]

Yet another type of preference-distortion problem arises when one party has direct responsibility for another and may not properly consider the other's utility. Margolis discusses this case with respect to education, in which the parent is concerned for his child's future economic and social well-being, but that we still do not accept the parent's full control over his child's education.[31] He suggests, "We have strained ourselves in the search for externality effects, many of which can be interpreted as parental 'inadequate' demand for education of his child."[32] Margolis asks if willingness to impose on the parent's judgments concerning financing education should be extended to other public services.

A similar case can be made for mental health care, especially when consumption of the service by a dependent is involved. The merit argument in the case of intrafamily distribution of utilities suggests that it is socially desirable for the service to be publicly provided and that the service receive public financial support. This reasoning applies especially to services for children and

---

[f]A number of studies have demonstrated that consumer ignorance is inversely related to income; that the poor tend to have less information on which to base consumption decisions than do members of higher income groups.[29]

[g]This analysis suggests the presence of a "time" externality, a notion similar to that for including interperiod considerations in constructing a rate of discount and in ascribing costs and benefits to those points in time when they are incurred. The counterpart of a spatial externality, it indicates that the implications of alternative courses of action at one point in time on costs and benefits at another point in time are not explicitly accounted for in utility or production functions.

youth, and in part to services for elderly and for those persons who are dependent because of disability. Mandatory consumption still raises major legal and ethical problems, but where resistance is primarily from the parents, intervention may be more easily justified.

Distributional Problems

This feature of merit goods, as noted by Head, has been discussed at length in welfare economics, but this discussion has failed to result in any consensus. Yet redistribution of income is a common rationale for public provision of merit goods and is a basis for defining some goods as meritorious.[h]

Distribution can have several dimensions; through time, over space, and between individuals or groups. Earlier discussion in this chapter of the first two of these dimensions primarily emphasized the problems which they caused in determining when and how public services should be provided and by what governmental unit in order to internalize extraconsumer effects. The subject of special interest here is intergroup transfers, in part as a means toward achieving equity in income and consumption of certain goods.

Hirsch identifies five urban governmental services that have important income redistributing qualities: education, public welfare, public health services, public housing, and public hospitals.[34] This list implicity includes mental health services, the redistributive character of which is furthered by the tendency of higher income groups to seek individual therapy in the private sector. Similarly, part of the private good value of public mental health services is captured when user charges are employed and are based on ability to pay.

As Samuelson points out,[35] a purpose of programs such as mental health services being called merit goods is that they may be used for redistributive transfers *in kind*, and that this is a subtle, political expedient since there is less resistance to this than to money transfers.[i] By interfering with comsumer sovereignty, transfers in kind distort consumers' preferences and would appear to complicate the problem of identifying social and individual optimal allocations of resources. However, Margolis argues that after an optimal

---

[h]Tiebout and Houston differentiate between merit and "necessity" goods, the latter appearing only in Musgrave's "distribution" budget, and constituting high priority private wants or needs. They argue that merit goods are not essentially for redistribution; that, with equal distribution of income, housing and medical care as examples would no longer be merit goods. As does Musgrave, they argue that local efforts to modify federal definitions of "proper" redistribution would lead to unstable results, or in other words, that redistribution is properly a federal rather than a local function.[33]

[i]Tiebout and Houston argue that the rich will tolerate a higher unfavorable net residuum, i.e., their benefits less their taxes for the service, if the transfer is in the form of a necessity good rather than a "pure" transfer. They observe, however, that it is politically easier to argue for a *social* rather than a *necessity* good.[36]

combination of income and merit goods transfers is arrived at, these transfers are viewed by the recipients as constraints within which consumers seek to optimize, which theoretically would facilitate reaching a Pareto optimum.[37]

An aspect of the argument for achieving redistribution by publicly providing certain meritorious goods is the ideological stance that citizens should have equal access to such basic goods as mental health services.[38] As medical care has come to be accepted as a right, though this has seldom been implemented, so availability of mental health services is coming to be regarded as a right. In other words, mental health services are gaining high social priority among the range of public and private services available to consumers, with the consequence that they are considered as merit goods[39] for purposes of justifying public intervention in their supply.[j] Where informational and other costs vary with socioeconomic groups, the principle of equal access suggests these costs should be equalized through differential pricing and design of the delivery system serving each of these groups.

Public Goods Problems

Head's third category of problems to which merit goods respond involves extraconsumer effects from using some kinds of services. Direct and even second-round spillovers of a relatively conventional economic sort were discussed earlier, and we have seen that a merit good is primarily private in nature yet possesses some features of collective consumption.

Tiebout and Houston have chosen to define merit or "interference" goods as possessing primarily *psychic* externalities, as differentiated from those discussed earlier.[41] These are goods the consumption of which is thought "good for the individual," and that higher levels of individual consumption resulting from public subsidy and regulation would yield "psychic income" to the citizenry. This is one way of defining a good as being affected with the public interest. Thus the individual's utility function takes into *account* other people's consumption of a merit good, but is perhaps not as directly affected by this as is the case when more objective, conventional and perhaps more tangible external effects of consumption exist.

Concerning mental health service, we may reason that citizens gain satisfaction from seeing disabled people receive treatment or are troubled by seeing untreated disability.[42] Where income redistribution is also involved, interest in charity or civic spirit may be considered an external effect. Margolis observes that the privileged may allocate some of their resources to providing additional income or specific goods for the underprivileged by way of charity. However, if charity is not motivated by grace of giving but by a more general

[j]Equal quality of public services over jurisdictions is a related piece of public ideology, which Margolis sees as a "halo effect" from our legal principle of equal protection.[40]

interest in the welfare of the underprivileged, charity is a public good. This does not invalidate charity as a basis for identifying a good as meritorious, but it does further complicate efforts to identify a Pareto optimum.[43]

Conclusion

The major purpose of this discussion has been to analyze mental health care from a welfare economics perspective in order to identify how this service should be designed and whether it should be publicly or privately provided. Consumer interdependence, the role of uncertainty, and the merit good qualities of psychotherapy have been investigated. It appears that, while mental health services are affected by the first two of these to the extent that public intervention is justified, that these services are properly primarily considered as merit goods. Public encouragement of their consumption through subsidy is indicated, and this subsidy should be allocated in such a manner that consumption will not vary on the basis of socioeconomic group membership, as for example by age or family income.

For mental health services to be made effectively equally accessible to all, differences in the real costs faced by different consumer groups, even when the good is provided without user charge, will have to be considered in designing and delivering the services. Development of operational criteria to guide such design is complicated by perceptual or "subjective" differences among consumers and thus by the very problems in securing true revealed preferences which constitute a major argument for public provision of mental health services. Some of these problems may be overcome by analyzing the recorded behavior of clients using subsidized outpatient mental health services. The second half of this study reports on empirical work using this strategy.

5

Westside Mental Health Center: A Case Study

We have discussed previous empirical work on consumer behavior in response to ways in which health and mental health services are provided, and the nature and welfare features of community mental health services. Treatment of these subjects provides the basis for further empirical work toward developing an understanding of the influence of various supply characteristics on utilization of clinical mental health services. The research reported here involves a case study, employing collection and analysis of client data for a major community mental health program. The procedures used are further discussed in the following three chapters. The purposes of this chapter are to functionally define the organization, context, and population of the case study.

This investigation analyzes the behavior of people consuming clinical mental health services provided by the Westside Community Mental Health Center of San Fransiso, California. The catchment area, called Westside Community Mental Health District, corresponds spatially to Health District Two as defined by the San Francisco Department of Public Health.

Approximately five square miles in size, Westside District is located in the northwestern portion of the city. It includes the area from Van Ness Avenue to Sixth Avenue and Stanyan Street, and from Market Street and Seventeenth to the waterfront at the Marina. The population, a total of 157,543 people in 1960, includes members of all racial groups and socioeconomic classes living in San Francisco.

The following section briefly analyzes the services and organization of the community mental health program in San Francisco and specifically that of the Westside Center. A general treatment of characteristics of the population residing in the Westsid District is followed by an analysis of the sociospatial structure of the catchment. These sections provide information important to understanding the clientele for therapeutic services in this section of the city.

Data collection procedures and a general discussion of attributes of these data define the basis for analyzing observed consumer behavior. The first analysis of this data presents the geographical distribution of people using clinical services, by areas defined as sociospatial units of the Westside District.

Organization and Provision of Mental Health Services in San Francisco and the Westside District

Public provision of psychiatric assistance to residents of San Francisco is the

57

responsibility of the city and county Department of Public Health. Community Mental Health Services is one of the three major program branches of the department, along with Public Health Services and Hospital Services. In conformance with state requirements, the program for the city is overseen by the Mental Health Advisory Board which is appointed by the Board of Supervisors and consists of seven members, at least one of whom must be a lay member.

The mental health program is financed by the city and county of San Francisco and has been partially reimbursed by Short-Doyle funds, administered by the California Department of Mental Hygiene, for psychiatric services to residents who could not afford private services. State monies supplemented fees paid by patients on a sliding scale based on their income.

Federal support of the program in San Francisco has taken the form of National Institute of Mental Health grants to projects in several of the health districts in the city. These grants have supported a psychiatric residency program, construction of some community mental health center facilities, and staffing grants to several health districts.

For purposes of administration, San Francisco has been divided into five health districts, each having approximately equal populations. These districts were adopted as the basis for providing community mental health services, and interviews with the directors of programs for four of these revealed that the districts exercise almost complete autonomy in their program design and operation. Health District Two defines the area used as the catchment for the Westside Community Mental Health Center.

The Westside Community Mental Health Center, Inc. is a public nonprofit corporation. After receiving a five-year, $1.6 million staffing grant from the federal government, it began operations on January 1, 1969. The range of services provided by the Westside Center is designed to meet federal requirements for a community mental health program as discussed in Chapter 3. The annual budget of the center is a little over $2 million.

The Westside Center is unusual in that it was formed as a confederation of private agencies which had been providing mental health services. Agencies which established the consortium were four hospitals: Children's Hospital and Adult Medical Center, Mount Zion Hospital and Medical Center, Pacific Presbyterian Medical Center, and Saint Mary's Hospital and Medical Center; two family service agencies: Jewish Family Service and Family Service Agency of San Francisco; the California Medical Clinic for Pyschotherapy; Suicide Prevention of San Francisco which is located near the District; and Conard House, a halfway facility.

The four hospitals and Conard House previously had contracts with the city and county of San Francisco for supplying diagnostic and treatment services to people who qualified for state payments under the Short-Doyle Act. These agencies continued to have contracts covering people not residing in the catchment, but the Westside Center became the contractor for providing treatment for Westside District residents. Each member agency of the Westside Center continues to treat private as well as subsidized patients.

Seven additional agencies located in the Westside District have joined the consortium since its establishment. These include Catholic Social Service; Baker Place and Progress House; Saint Elizabeth's Infant Hospital; and The Drug Treatment Program at 409-½ Clayton Street, Reality House West and Walden House, all of which offer drug treatment programs.

Only psychiatric outpatient, inpatient and partial hospitalization services have qualified for Short-Doyle reimbursement for patient care. Many of the agencies which are members of the Westside Center receive no public monies. The Laterman-Petris-Short Act was to have supported patient care at halfway houses and residential drug treatment facilities, but the program has not been funded.[a]

Available Psychiatric Services

Agencies which are members of the consortium operate at locations scattered through the Westside District. Augmented with a few services initiated by the Westside Center, they together provide the range of services required by federal legislation for a comprehensive community mental health program. The following are services supplied by the various agencies which are members of the Westside Center.

1. Adult Emergency

   The Crisis Clinic, adjoining the emergency room at Mt. Zion Hospital

2. Child Emergency

   McAuley Neuropsychiatric Institute, St. Mary's Hospital

3. Adult Outpatient

   California Medical Clinic for Psychotherapy
   Children's Hospital and Adult Medical Center
   Mt. Zion Hospital and Medical Center
   Pacific Presbyterian Medical Center
   McAuley Institute at St. Mary's Hospital and Medical Center

4. Child Outpatient

   Children's Hospital
   Mt. Zion Hospital
   Pacific Presbyterian Hospital
   St. Mary's Hospital

---

[a]The five residential centers together commonly accommodate around ninety people, who on the average stay about three months. Some residents use day treatment and other therapeutic services while living at one of these centers.

5. Adult Inpatient and Partial Hospitalization on the ward

   Mt. Zion Hospital
   Pacific Presbyterian Hospital
   St. Mary's Hospital

6. Child Inpatient and Partial Hospitalization on the ward

   St. Mary's Hospital

7. Adult Rehabilitation (Nondrug)

   Day Treatment Center at Pacific Presbyterian Hospital
   Conard House
   Baker Place
   Progress House

8. Child and Adolescent Rehabilitation

   Mt. Zion Hospital
   St. Mary's Hospital

9. Drug Treatment

   Crisis Clinic (outpatient)
   Drug Treatment Program (outpatient)
   Reality House West (residential)
   Walden House (residential)

10. Casework and Family Counseling

    Family Service Agency of San Francisco
    Jewish Family Service Agency
    Catholic Social Service

11. Maternity Service for Unwed Mothers

    St. Elizabeth's Infant Hospital

12. Telephone Emergency Service

    Suicide Prevention of San Francisco

13. Home Visitation

    Mt. Zion Hospital

14. Community Consultation

    California Medical Clinic for Psychotherapy
    Mt. Zion Hospital
    Westside Central Office

15. Education and Training

    Westside Central Office

16. Research and Evaluation

    Westside Central Office

The Crisis Clinic at Mt. Zion Hospital provides adult emergency care on a twenty-four hour, seven day a week basis, a drug withdrawal program of daily counseling, and short-term therapy up to six outpatient visits. It also serves as the central referral agency for the Westside Center. Outpatients may be admitted by the Crisis Clinic, receive therapy there, and then be referred for additional therapy to a regular outpatient clinic. Approximately 9.3 percent of the patients admitted during three sample months representing 1969/70 in this study reported that they were referred by the Crisis Clinic to one of the five outpatient units in the district. Most individuals using outpatient services go directly to the outpatient unit of their choosing and, based on evaluation, are admitted to that unit without having visited the Crisis Clinic.

The Crisis Clinic controls all referrals to inpatient services for Westside residents, assigning clients needing hospitalization to the various inpatient units on the basis of available beds. This results in a largely random and even distribution of Westside District patients by place of residence using each of the inpatient units.

While the length of outpatient therapy provided by Westside Center is not limited, inpatients are permitted only fourteen days of hospitalization a year. The Crisis Clinic and Westside Center inpatient units may refer a patient to California State Hospital at Napa for more extensive hospitalization. These agencies may also refer patients to the California State Hospital at Mendocino for residential drug treatment, but not all referred patients are accepted for admission. The San Francisco Community Mental Health Program is billed for patients treated at state hospitals. Shortage of local funds has led to efforts at avoiding use of state hospitals as well as to the limits on inpatient care provided by the Westside Center, and has encouraged development of alternatives to hospitalization.[b]

Governance

Westside Community Mental Health Center, Inc. is governed by a Board of Directors consisting of two representatives from each of the sixteen member agencies and sixteen members of the Community Advisory Board.[c] One

---

[b]General cost figures used by Westside Center in 1970 included: $29.94 per individual interview unit (hour), $29.39 per partial hospitalization day, $27.85 per partial care (day care) day, $12.83 per residential care (halfway house) day, and $104.97 per full hospitalization (24 hour) day. Full hospitalization, which is more expensive from Westside Center inpatient units than from state hospitals, is provided in the hope that the patients's tenure will be short, and that continued contact with the community and family will have therapeutic value. During 1969/70, 46 percent of the Westside Center budget was spent on hospitalization. Since relatively few people are served by this expenditure, there is great interest on the part of some Westside Center staff to somehow reduce hospitalization and consequently free monies for funding other services.

[c]The Community Advisory Board is composed of individuals who are intended to represent

representative from each agency is a clinical or administrative staff member and the other is a member of the board of directors of the agency. Each member agency has only one vote, thus dividing the voting representation equally between agencies providing mental health services and community representatives.

The Board of Directors has policy and fiscal responsibility for the program. It is expected to adopt and oversee implementation of policies considered essential for coordinating the functions of the member agencies as well as regulations assuring continuity of care and accountability of professional staff. The Board of Directors selects a medical director whose responsibilities include employing the staff and overseeing the operations of Central Office, and developing the program of the Westside Center within the policies adopted by the board. Perhaps predictably, financial problems have been a major focus of concern for the board since the establishment of the Westside Center. This preoccupation and limited information concerning the current use of services and mental health status of Westside District residents have resulted in little attention being given to program planning.

The board established several committees in early 1970, with functional responsibilities such as program planning and development of the budget. The personnel committee, which reviews applicants for positions at the Central Office and at member agencies when these involve Westside Center funding, has been especially active and the center of substantial contention. Most of the more heated conflicts in committees and at meetings of the Board of Directors have involved specific expenditures, a specific service, or in the case of the personnel committee, the race and apparent attitude of prospective employees.

When asked for their evaluation of the power exercised by the Board of Directors, members of the board who thought that it was influential based their judgment on its ability to obtain supplemental funding from the San Francisco Board of Supervisors during a period of tight budgets. Agency representatives to this board who are directors of large hospitals were also considered to exercise considerable influence in securing the support of these hospitals for Westside Center programs. Board members commonly expressed concern for the lack of direction and articulated purposes guiding the efforts of the Westside Center. Some were also concerned that because services are provided at a number of locations in the area, no one in particular knows what is going on everywhere.

Board members differed in their perception of the power they individually had in decisions made by the board. Many of the professionals representing member agencies judged that representatives from the Community Advisory

---

the residents of the Westside District. The functions of this organization include identifying community needs, acting as an advocate of consumer interests, and assessing the performance of mental health services. This board expresses its findings to the member agencies and to the Board of Directors. Several members of the Advisory Board are employed by the Westside Center, especially in its Central Office.

Board had exceptional power and had completely determined the direction which the Westside Center has taken.

Agencies Providing Clinical Services

In this investigation, we are primarily concerned with clinical services and especially those provided to adult patients. In the case of the Westside Center, these services almost entirely take the form of individual interview sessions usually running one hour in length. Two major kinds of clinical service are available to residents of the Westside District; immediate, short-term therapy available at any time at the Crisis Clinic, and longer-term therapy of the more conventional psychiatric form which is provided by the five outpatient centers.

Several of the functions performed by the Crisis Clinic have already been discussed. Centrally located in the Westside District, it deals with both emergency psychiatric problems and appears to be the agency chosen as the major source of nonemergency service by people who are seeking psychiatric service but who do not want to wait for admission or to have to make a personal commitment to therapy.

Of the five agencies providing traditional individual outpatient services, only California Medical Clinic for Psychotherapy is not located in a hospital facility also offering medical services. California Clinic is a private facility established by psychiatric social workers and others to supply long-term therapy. Most of the patients are middle-class people who pay for, or have insurance covering, the service. While its patients, especially referrals, are recorded with the Westside Center Central Office, California Clinic received no Short-Doyle funds. This is the only agency in the Westside District with a waiting list of professionals wanting to work or to train there.

Children's Hospital is the only member agency with an outpatient clinic but no inpatient services. Along with St. Mary's, Children's has no waiting list. Walkin clients will usually receive an appointment for within the next twenty-four hours. The outpatient clinic at Pacific Presbyterian will also give an early appointment to clients, but had until recently a long intake procedure involving three days of diagnostic testing before a person was admitted to therapy. In contrast, the outpatient clinic at Mt. Zion usually has a waiting list of from one to three weeks. Black residents of the Westside District decided to use Mt. Zion outpatient as their primary center for this service, and concentrated community effort toward obtaining relevant services here in the hope of causing this agency to develop special competence in dealing with the problems of black patients.

The Population of the Westside District

Demographically, the Westside District is most easily characterized by its racial, social, and economic diversity. This section provides a brief overview of the characteristics of people residing in the catchment area. This population is the universe for much of the analysis which follows.[d]

Westside District consists of thirty-three census tracts (see Figure 5-1). It includes Census Area B, which occupies roughly the northern third of the catchment, and Census Area J, which accounts for most of the southern two-thirds of the catchment. Additional Census Tracts D1 and H1 are located at the western edge of the Westside District.[e] The 1960 enumerated population of the Westside District by racial groups reported in census tract data included 104,044 Caucasians (66 percent), 35,079 black people (22.3 percent), 6,065 Mexican-Americans (3.9 percent), and 12,355 other people (7.8 percent). Census figures for 1970 show that the total population of the district was 147,357, a decline of over 10,000 residents during that decade.

The population of Census Area B is almost totally Caucasian, with the exception of Tract B9 in which 22 percent of the residents are black. Median family income of the population in this area ranges from $7,316 to $18,281, substantially higher than for the city as a whole (S.F.: median family income was $6,717). All tracts in Area B have median years of schooling above 12.0, and 20 percent to 33 percent of the adult populations in seven tracts had completed four years of college (S.F.: median years completed was 12.0, and population completing four years of college was 11 percent). Occupationally, all tracts in this area had at least one-third of the working residents in professional-managerial jobs (S.F.: 23.1 percent), while ten tracts had more than 40 percent of these residents in this category.

In contrast, the twenty-one tracts in Census Area J had black populations ranging from 22.1 percent to 68.0 percent, with seven of the tracts exceeding 50 percent (S.F.: 10.1 percent of the population was black). Japanese, while not enumerated in census tract data, probably account for most of the one-fifth and one-fourth of the population classified racially as "other" in Census Tracts J2 and J6.

Approximately 90 percent of the population in Census Area J has a median family income range of $3,463 to $6,649, which is below that for San Francisco. Twelve tracts have median schooling for the population of below twelve years,

---

[d]Population base figures used in most of the analysis are taken from the 1960 U.S. Census of Population. This was found to be necessary because at the time that most of the data analysis was performed, only total population figures by census tract for the 1970 Census had been released.

[e]The Westside District boundaries include as well Tract C1 and portions of D2 and E1. Tract C1 is the Presidio military post which had no residents using Westside Center services during the time period examined. Although about 8 percent of Census Tracts D2 and E1 are included within a narrow western extention of the Westside District boundaries, from this area only four people residing in D2 were included in the sample months representing 1969-70. Because inclusion of the population figures for three tracts would bias analytical results, these three tracts are excluded from tabulations in this study.

and of the only six with higher levels of education than for the city, between 11.5 percent and 19.8 percent of the populations had completed four years of college. Only three tracts including 2 percent of the population in Area J have at least one-third of the working adults in professional-managerial positions.

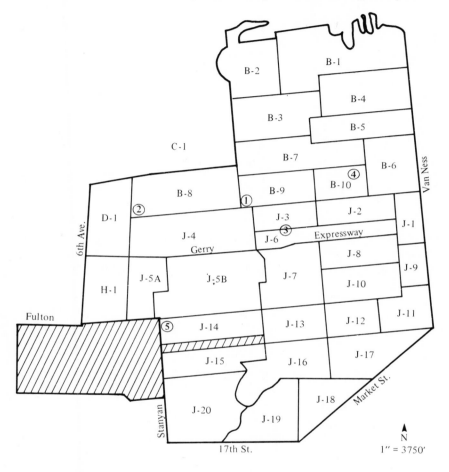

1. California Medical Clinic for Psychotherapy
2. Children's Hospital
3. Mount Zion Hospital and the Crisis Clinic
4. Pacific Presbyterian Medical Center
5. St. Mary's Hospital
J-1, B-5, etc. designate Census Tracts

Figure 5-1. The Westside District, San Francisco: Boundaries, Census Tracts, and the Location of Agencies Providing Clinical Services

Excluding Tract J19, from 40 percent to 75 percent of the working residents in tracts constituting Area J are skilled, unskilled and "other" laborers.

Census Areas B and J also differ in sex ratios and the marital status of residents. The sex ratio in Area B varies by tract from 66.9 to 75.4 percent, substantially below the 96.4 percentage rate for the city. Seven tracts in Area J have ratios higher than for the city, nine tracts have ratios between 90 and 100, and the remaining five vary from 77.2 to 86.2.

The proportion of males who are married is generally greater for tracts in Area B than for the city, while the female marital rate tends to be lower. Tracts with relatively high single male and female rates are located around Pacific Presbyterian Medical Center and in the high-rent apartment area of Pacific-Heights.

Seventeen of the tracts in Area J have single male rates which fall between 32 percent and 46 percent, all of which are higher than the city rate of 31.9 percent. Fourteen of these tracts had lower proportions of single females (15.8 to 22.2 percent versus 22.7 percent) than for the city as a whole. The separation rate for males and females showed the same pattern of spatial distribution, with all but one tract having rates for males between 2.3 and 20.5 percent, all higher than the city rate which was 2 percent of all males ever married. The rate is higher still for females, with all but two tracts falling between 4.9 and 19.3 percent.

Finally, these two major portions of the Westside District also differ in the age and fertility characteristics of their populations. Median ages of females for tracts in Area B ranged from 36 to 53, and for males from 33 to 49 (S.F.: female median age 50.9, male 49.1). The median age of women in a majority of B tracts was beyond the childbearing age of 44, and in eight tracts above that for male residents. All but one tract has a higher proportion of persons 65 years of age and over than the 12.6 percent rate for the city as a whole.

While the population of Area B tends to exceed in age the profile for the city, the population of Area J is younger than that for the city, with large proportions of both sexes within the age range for childbearing. The median age of females for tracts in Area J ranged from 31 to 51, with the median for sixteen tracts under 40 years. The medians for males ranged from 31 to 49 years, with nineteen tracts having a median under 40 years. Ten of the tracts in this area had fertility rates in excess of 336.36 per thousand women 15-44 years of age, the rate for San Francisco. Three tracts, which also predominately consisted of black residents, had fertility rates one-third greater than the rate for the city.

This general analysis of census tract data for the 1960 population provides a demographic summary of the people living in the Westside District. While the area has witnessed considerable changes in population over the last decade as a result of urban renewal and other influences, these changes have been most pronounced in Census Area J. The general findings presented here probably still reasonably typify these two census areas, especially their demographic differences.

The Sociospatial Structure of Westside District

Westside District includes residents from all socioeconomic groups and most of the racial groups living in San Francisco. While virtually every portion of the district includes some variety of population on these bases, residents and professionals working in the area observe a spatial distribution of social groups structured as a set of residential areas. These areas tend to be delimited by major streets, changes in topography, and open spaces. They are inhabited by relatively homogeneous populations.

While it could be inadvisable to use these areas as the basis for providing some residentially oriented public services, they do provide a basis for describing the spatial dimension of the social structure in Westside and for analyzing some of the data on current use of mental health services. The areas are seen as sociological "territories," both in perceptions of residents and in a demographic sense.[f] For purposes of this study, these areas were delimited by aggregating census tracts into areas commonly occupied by a single locality group although in some cases these are occupied by several social groups.

The Western Addition is generally bounded by California and Fulton Streets, and by Van Ness Avenue and Baker Street. It is a major black ghetto of San Francisco. Although portions of the area are racially integrated, the population is primarily black, except for a concentrated area north of Geary housing much of the Japanese and Korean communities of San Francisco.

The Western Addition is a major Economic Opportunity Target Area and the location for much of the urban redevelopment activity in the city. Redevelopment has accounted for substantial changes in the population of this area over the last decade, with the recent location of expensive apartments for the retired and town houses for middle-income families on Cathedral Hill. Geary Expressway divides the Western Addition visually and functionally. Consequently, it is analytically useful to differentiate the tracts lying north and south of this traffic artery.

Area 1. This area, which we shall refer to as Western Addition North, consists of census tracts J1 through 3, and J6. It includes the Japanese and Korean communities, most of Cathedral Hill, and some white residents especially in the blocks along Pine and Bush Streets.

Area 2. Western Addition South consists of census tracts J7 through 10. It

---

[f]Suttles, in his study of the Addams area in Chicago, develops the concept of territorially segregated "locality groups" as a dimension of social structure. This is an extension of the earlier notion of "natural areas," originating with the work of Park and Burgess and criticized on the basis of its "physicalistic terminology."[1] Demographically, the set of areas defined in this study reflect the concepts developed by Shevsky and Bell, but seek to avoid the criticisms of Hawley and Duncan by considering the limitations of census tracts as boundaries of residential groups and by using local functional definitions rather than merely empirical abstractions.[2]

includes "The Fillmore," a several block section along Fillmore Street with a high incidence of drug addiction and prostitution, and several integrated low-cost housing projects. The population is almost entirely black and low income.

Area 3. The area adjacent to Western Addition on the south consists of tracts J12 through 14 and is bounded by Van Ness, Oak Street and the Panhandle of Golden Gate Park, Stanyan and Fulton Streets. Known as Alamo Plaza, this is primarily an integrated working class area with a substantial number of young people, experimenting with alternative life-styles. These tracts include parts of the University of San Francisco with a related staff and student population in the west, and the eastern end has traditionally been the home of lower-middle-income white immigrants from the rural southern United States.

Area 4. The area south of the Panhandle is known is the Haight-Ashbury. It includes census tracts J15 through 17 and is bounded on the south by Waller and Duboce. In the early 1960s, this was an increasingly black transitional neighborhood, which then became an internationally known center of the hippie community in San Francisco. Most of the white "street people" and residential communes have now left the area and the population is approximately 30 percent black lower income and working class.

Area 5. Buena Vista Heights occupies the slopes of Olympus and Corona south of the Haight. Consisting of census tracts J19 and 20, it is bounded on the south by 17th Street and runs from Stanyan to Castro. This is an old, upper-middle-income neighborhood, which is now predominately occupied by young professionals and families with young to middle-aged heads of households. It is a racially integrated area, and many of the populations have a higher education. The political and social values of the population tend to be liberal, in contrast to the conservatism found in the Pacific Heights.

Area 6. This is the northern most portion of Westside, known as the Marina. The almost exclusively white population consists of young, often unmarried business and professional people, and of retired people who are often widowed. This population enjoys a higher standard of living than their incomes would suggest, largely because their incomes tend to be less than they will be or have been. Rents are relatively high, supported by the status, amenities, and accommodations provided in the area. The Marina consists of tracts B1 through 5 and is bounded on the south by Green and Vallejo Streets.

Area 7. Pacific Heights and Presidio Heights occupy a ridge south of the Marina. These are among the highest income sections of San Francisco, consisting of large single-family houses, expensive apartments, and a few residential clubs for young single people. Several private schools and most of the consulates in the city are located here. The population is almost entirely white. Area 7 includes census tracts B6 through 8 and is bounded on the south by Jackson between Lyon and Laguna Streets, and by California in the eastern and western portions of the area.

Area 8. Census tracts B9 and B10 constitute a largely middle-class, integrated area with a black and white population. The Alta Plaza area is a transition zone which, while sometimes considered part of the Western Addition, is relatively well maintained. Upper-middle-class families with professional heads of household are beginning to move into some of the large single-family houses in the area, especially adjacent and to the west of the square.

Area 9. The Inner Richmond area is at the western edge of Westside and consists of census tracts D1, D2, E1, H1, and J5A. It shows some of the middle-class attributes of Area 8, but its integration is primarily Chinese and white with some Filipino residents. Incomes are slightly higher, and the population is somewhat more conservative and appears more upwardly mobile than residents of Alta Plaza.

Area 10. Three census tracts, occupying two portions of Westside, defy the general characterization of populations possible for the other areas. Two of these, J4 and J5B, vary from the almost entirely white and Chinese Inner Richmond area to the largely unintegrated black population of Western Addition. The third tract is J18, in the southeastern corner of Westside. This area contains several populations, including primarily white older-middle-class couples and young people who identify with the counterculture living immediately east of Corona Heights. The lower portion of the tract, toward Market Street, has a mixed population of black and white residents and some people with Spanish surnames.

While the populations of these two areas are not highly similar, the areas are especially heterogeneous and difficult to typify. Consequently, for purposes of this analysis, these three tracts have been combined.

The ten areas which we have typified and briefly discussed generally characterize the spatial distribution of various populations residing in Westside. They point up the racial and socioeconomic diversity of the area. They also reveal a general pattern; a largely black ghetto surrounded by transitional areas which physically separate a periphery of higher income residential areas. This outer band of more expensive housing is in turn quite differentiated, both in social characteristics of the population and in physical characteristics of housing types and topography. As a more highly aggregated overview, Westside may be typified as having two major populations which are divided by a hill. The northern section of the district, consisting of the B census tracts, has a middle and upper class, primarily white population. The southern section, including the J census tracts, contains a proportionately Larger young and over sixty-five population which has lower incomes, less education, and consists of blacks, Japanese, and whites. The spatial distribution pattern of this diverse population is useful in understanding the structure of the district and in assessing the differential use of community mental health services.

The Data on Westside Center Clients

Data on consumer characteristics and behavior in using clinical services provided by Westside Center were collected from a series of clinical and administrative records dealing with patient transactions and services. The major objectives in selecting patients for data-collection purposes were to avoid double counting and to secure a sample of observations representing the incidence of treated mental illness during two time periods.

This was done by first randomly selecting two sample months, March and October, which would be used for each time period. These are also distributed over the year in such a manner that they account for recognized seasonal variation in demand. Data was then collected for March and October 1968, the year preceeding the establishment of the Westside Community Mental Health Center, Inc., and for March and October 1969, and March 1970. Data for the first two months are used to represent the client and use patterns for 1968, and data for the second three months are used to represent the same features for the first year and a half of Westside Center's operation.

To account for the incidence of treated illness, only those clients who were first admitted to one of the clinical services during a sample month were selected as observations.[g] Names, patient numbers, and some demographic information for these clients were obtained from the log books of each of the six agencies supplying clinical services.

Having identified the clients of outpatient services which would constitute the full set of observations, five additional sets of records were consulted to obtain the full range of available information concerning the characteristics, use of services including readmission, and psychiatric condition of these individuals.[h] Strict confidentiality was maintained, and all materials which could be

---

[g]The numbers of observations for outpatient first admissions during the sample months was as follows:

March 1968	95	October 1969	431
October 1968	108	March 1970	413
March 1969	258		

[h]Data on each observation included eighteen items, including information on eight demographic variables and ten variables dealing with characteristics of the service consumed such as the place, date, type and length of therapy, and so forth. Information on some

used to link a patient record with an individual were destroyed as soon as the record was complete.

The additional sets of records which were consulted were redundant concerning a number of data items, but this permitted rechecking the information which was collected. The additional sources included Statewide Uniform Data System forms on individual patient information required by the California Department of Mental Hygiene, Request and Authorization forms for Short-Doyle funding required by the San Francisco Community Mental Health Program, and the Westside Center Patient Logbook, which is the register of all patients using services of agencies belonging to Westside Center and maintained by the Central Office. The Westside Patient Transactional Card File, a current central file of clients used for reference by the member clinics and updated on an almost daily basis, was consulted for verifying and augmenting the other records on each patient drawn as an observation. Finally, billing records of Westside Center were used to confirm whether clients were still in service and the mode of payment used.

The data-collection phase of this research required almost four months of more than full-time work. Data for this project has also been employed to develop informational reports for use in program planning by the Westside Center, which was a basis of the cooperation received from the Central Office. Comparable information for inpatients for the five sample months was also collected.

All data was digitized, punched on to cards, and became the basis for the analysis reported in sections of this and the following chapters. This data appears to be the most complete and extensive of its sort for any area in the western United States.

The Proportional Spatial Distribution of Outpatient Service Users

Using the data on consumers who were first admitted to outpatient service during the five sample months, counts were made of those using each of the six agencies providing this service from each of the ten areas of Westside, described earlier in this chapter.

The highest proportion of outpatients admitted by each of the agencies except the Crisis Clinic came from outside the Westside catchment, and ranged from 73.2 percent of the St. Mary to 30.7 percent of the Children's Hospital intake. It should be recalled that these agencies also have Short-Doyle contracts

---

observations ran to forty-four data items, including data on up to three readmissions. The set of patient records did not provide data on education, occupation or ethnic group membership other than race, all variables which are desirable for differentiating consumer groups.

with the city to serve patients living in other portions of San Francisco, except for the Crisis Clinic which is intended solely for Westside residents, and California Medical Clinic for Psychotherapy (Cal. Med.), which receives money from a federal staffing grant but no Short-Doyle funds. Non-Westside patients account for 42 percent of all patients served by agencies belonging to Westside Center.

The area within Westside with the greatest number of service users is the Haight (11.2 percent), followed by Alamo (9.3 percent), Western Addition South (7.4 percent) and North (6.1 percent), and Buena Vista (5.5 percent) (N = 1305). The Crisis Clinic sees the highest proportion of clients from each of these five areas, with the highest proportion of clients coming from the Haight (21.9 percent), the area with the greatest number of outpatient clients (145) during the five sample months. The proportionate contribution by the population of the various areas to Crisis Clinic intake is in the same rank order as the order of areas by frequency of use of all outpatient services. Among the other agencies, only Mt. Zion Hospital and Cal. Med. have highest proportions of clients (7.1 percent, 6.4 percent) from the area which also has the highest frequency of use, the Haight.[i] As might be expected, the area in which St. Mary's is located (Area 3) accounts for the highest proportion (7.6 percent, N = 251) of outpatients using that facility. Pacific Presbyterian (PMC), Children's Hospital, and Mt. Zion unusually high proportions of outpatients from Western Addition South, in numbers accounting for the largest or second largest source of clients in each case.

PMC receives its greatest number of patients from Buena Vista (Area 5), which involves traveling considerably further than would be required in using either St. Mary's or Mt. Zion. Children's Hospital and Cal. Med., which are spatially further from Buena Vista than from any of the other four high frequency use areas, draw their largest number of outpatients from this area. Mt. Zion outpatient clinic receives proportionately fewer clients from Western Addition North, the area in which it is located, than from three physically more distant areas. This may in part be explained by realizing that 69 percent of the outpatients from the adjacent blocks (Area 1) use the Crisis Clinic, which is located in the same building as is Mt. Zion outpatient.

Patients from each of the five remaining residential areas constituted less than 5 percent of the total first admissions to Westside agencies during the five sample months. The relative frequencies with which these patients used each of the agencies providing outpatient services are similar to those reported above.

---

[i]Because the Crisis Clinic opened in 1969, all data on use are for the last three sample months. Complete client records for the two 1968 sample months were not available for St. Mary's outpatient service, thus user figures for this period are not included in these calculations. Other records indicate that new admissions of Westside residents to St. Mary's for these months numbered 23 (21 white, 2 black) and that total first admissions including non-Westside residents were approximately 100.

Use patterns from the analysis which is briefly described here demonstrate some attenuating influence of distance and of intervening opportunity on the relative frequency of admissions at those agencies most distant from the residential area of the outpatient. Also, relative proportional use of a center by clients from several residential areas suggests that distance inversely affects use. However, anomalies to this pattern are almost as common, suggesting that several other factors exercise considerable influence on the process by which outpatient use is distributed among agencies.

Some additional general patterns emerge from this analysis. The Crisis Clinic, despite the fact that it operated for only three of the five sample months, saw substantially more outpatients from all areas, except Inner Richmond, than did any of the other agencies and was most intensively used by those residential areas with the largest numbers of outpatients.

Mt. Zion and St. Mary's are the agencies receiving the next greatest use by residents of the areas with high numbers of outpatients, seventeen of the twenty-one "J" census tracts.

Residential areas in the western portion of the catchment and north of California Street disproportionately use Children's Hospital, PMC, and Cal. Med., although these are not always among the closest facilities. With the exception of Buena Vista, these areas have the highest income populations in Westside. A pattern which emerges is that the generally lower-income residential areas of the Westside District make the most frequent use of outpatient services in the area and primarily tend to frequent a separate set of agencies than those preferred by the wealthier population in the northern and western portions of the catchment.

6

**Analysis of Consumer Behavior
with Respect to Attributes of
Clients and of Services Provided by
Westside Mental Health Center**

In this and the two following chapters, we are primarily concerned with analyzing the data on patients first admitted to Westside clinical services during five sample months representing the years 1968 through 1970. As explained in the previous chapter, these data deal both with client characteristics and their use of mental health services. The major purpose of this analysis is to begin to explain the choice and use of these services as a function of supply characteristics, and to do this for various consumer groups.

In other words, we are interested in identifying the influence of various features of clinical services, and the manner in which they are provided, on consumer demand. Further, we are interested in how these dimensions or attributes of mental health services differentially influence demand by groups of clients defined on the basis of their socioeconomic characteristics. In turn, we wish to identify means by which publicly provided clinical mental health services can be made more accessible and acceptable to these client groups, or to increase their real net benefit from consumption, to the end of more effectively satisfying both revealed and currently latent demand for therapeutic assistance.

The strategy used in this analysis involves a number of operations which are essentially sequential. Cross-tabulations on available data variables and measures of their nominal association[a] were examined in order to identify patterns of behavior by various client groups. A series of hypotheses, based on observations from four months of field work in the Westside catchment area and on reports

---

[a]Goodman-Kruskal's lambda is the primary measure of correlation or association used in this sudy.[1] Much of the following analysis deals with attribute data, which is nominal in scale. Small or zero cell frequencies in a number of the data matrices precluded using Chi square, another nominal level correlation coefficient.[2]

Goodman-Kruskal's lambda is a kind of correlation ratio, based on the nominal regression function consisting of a set of modal values.[3] Lambda may be defined as:

$$\lambda \text{ r.c.} = \frac{\sum_{j} \max_{i} N_{ij} - \max_{j} N_{.j}}{N - \max_{j} N_{.j}}$$

where the column variable is the independent or predictor variable.

The lambda coefficient indicates the gain in predictability on the basis of knowledge about the modes in the conditional distributions, rather than predicting on the basis of the marginal mode alone. The value of lambda may range from zero to one. A value of zero indicates that knowledge of the independent variable is of no assistance in predicting the dependent variable. A value of one (1.0) indicates that knowledge of the independent variable permits error free prediction of the dependent variable. The previously cited references provide a fuller discussion of this useful statistical technique.

of empirical work and hypotheses developed by other researchers, assisted in identifying promising tabulations.

Observation of patterns, concerning the distribution of use of a service center by racial groups, for example, then raised questions concerning the reasons for these patterns. Tentative explanations were sought, once again using field observations and the largely hypothetical work by others dealing with the delivery of mental health care. These explanations were then tested by applying additional information from the analysis of Westside data to confirm or reject the hypothesis. This process led as well to a number of deductions concerning desirable policy for use in designing a community mental health program. These policies were likewise tested using the analytical findings for Westside.[4]

This strategy was first applied using data on patients admitted during October 1969. General examination of the data revealed that this month reasonably represented patient distributions and behavior for the two sample months from 1969 and one month from 1970, the period immediately following the establishment of the Westside Mental Health Center, Inc. Most analysis was then repeated for combinations of the five sample months.

The search for aspects and explanations of consumer behavior in the use of Westside mental health services resulted in defining a series of questions which serve as a basis for organizing Chapters 6, 7, and 8. One of the first major questions is who uses these services. Answers begin to reveal differences in the behavior of individuals belonging to various consumer groups, especially proportionate underutilization, and to suggest possible ways of increasing equity in making services accessible and attractive to groups currently underrepresented among the patients served by Westside agencies.

A second major category of questions involves how people enter therapeutic care. Variation in the importance of sources of referral among client groups can suggest tactics for improving the access to services such as structuring programs to inform individuals or their counselors about when and where to seek assistance. These two sets of questions are addressed in the following sections of this chapter.

A third set of questions, which are dealt with in Chapter 7, relate to how agencies may be located to decrease the perceived costs of consumer trip-making. Our concern is with the influence of accessibility on consumer choice and utilization of outpatient and crisis mental health services. Our objectives are to identify the importance of distance on consumer behavior and appropriate ways of increasing accessibility when this has a critical effect on demand.

Chapter 8 deals with a closely related fourth set of questions, concerning the influence on consumer behavior of characteristics of the therapeutic service, as this service is supplied by various agencies. Of major interest are differences in demand for outpatient and crisis services, and the impact of the recently established Crisis Clinic on demand at outpatient clinics. We will also investigate the importance of differences among outpatient clinics in explaining consumer behavior.

General differences in the behavior of individuals belonging to various client groups are discussed in the following pages of this chapter, in the context of proportionate utilization of mental health services. However, specific intergroup differences with respect to the affect of distance and type of service, for example, are treated in Chapter 7. The interrelation of additional supply characteristics in influencing demand, the major subject of Chapter 8, similarly requires some disucssion of behavior patterns that are more typical of one group of clients than of another.

Classification of the analytical questions as just outlined does, however, provide a structure for the following chapters. These various attributes of the services provided, and the way in which they are provided, are seen as promising independent variables in consumer demand functions for the various groups which Westside Mental Health Center seeks to serve. Chapter 9 discusses an approach to developing such a consumer response model. While available data places limitations on identifying the relative importance and realtionships between these variables, the nature and to some extent the size of their impact is revealed by the analysis which follows. As pointed out by our discussion in Chapters 2 and 3 of previous research concerning psychiatric and medical health services, these findings constitute a substantial contribution to informing a user-oriented approach in planning for community mental health services.

Population Group Differences in Consuming Westside Clinical Mental Health Services

Who uses Westside outpatient mental health services? More specifically, of the patients first admitted during the sample months for which data was obtained, how do various groups of the client population proportionately utilize clinical psychiatric care? This information is basic to more detailed analysis of how various services are used, and facilitates identifying those groups which proportionately underutilize the services. Findings concerning the latter lead to further questions of why differential use occurs and how underrepresented groups might be better accommodated.

In this section, we will examine the extent to which various age, sex, race, and income groups use clinical services. We will also examine the distribution of patients by diagnosis. Finally, rates of withdrawal from service will be analyzed as an indicator of the extent to which current services are satisfactory in meeting effective demand.

Age Distribution of Use

Westside adult outpatients are predominately young, with the median age being twenty-five years. This general pattern holds both for the data from 1968 and from 1969/70. Further, more than 54 percent of the adult first admissions from 1968 sample months were between twenty-one and thirty years of age, while 47.8 percent of the new patients for the three months representing 1969/70 were from this age group. This age group accounted for half or more of the patients for most of the psychiatric clinics in Westside during both 1968 and 1969/70.[b]

While patients age thirty or younger constitute the majority of all adult clients for both time periods, the proportional distributions show a slight increase in users from each age category over thirty between 1968 and 1969/70. Most outpatient clinics have shared in the increase in patients over thirty. Over 43 percent of Children's Hospital outpatients are over thirty, while only 27.4 percent were from this age range in 1968. This agency began to serve adult outpatients in 1968, which largely explains the change in age distribution of its patients. Comparable figures for PMC are 32.5 and 28 percent. Similarly, 46 percent of St. Mary's patients were over thirty in 1969/70. However, California Medical Clinic for Psychotherapy (Cal. Med.) lost proportionately in this range, dropping from 31.9 to 28.2 percent.

Analysis of the age distribution for Mt. Zion is complicated because the ages for 19 percent of the 1969/70 sample were not recorded on clinical records. Of the patients for whom ages were recorded, Mt. Zion has proportionately lost patients from the age groups between sixteen and forty, while realizing an increase in patients from most older age groups. A possible explanation for these changes is the attractiveness of the Crisis Clinic, located in the same building, which served people between the ages of twenty-one and forty at rates higher than for the 1969/70 Westside clients as a whole. This explanation cannot be confirmed since the distribution of Mt. Zion patients for whom ages are not available could change the relative rates for these two agencies.

The age distribution of St. Mary's outpatients for 1969/70 differs from the figures for all other agencies. Roughly three-quarters of the patients using this agency are distributed in an almost even manner among the three youngest adult age groups; 21.1 percent are sixteen to twenty, 32.4 percent are twenty-one to thirty, and 20.6 percent are between thirty-one and forty years of age. Increases in the numbers of patients seen from age categories between forty-one and

---

[b]Patients younger than sixteen years are omitted from this analysis. Our primary concern is with adult patients using clinical services. Additionally, the data appears to underreport younger patients from Children's Hospital. Patients with ages zero through fifteen constitute 4.4 percent of all observations for 1968 and 7.1 percent for the months representing 1969/70. Over 73 percent of the observations for this age group from the latter time period used the clinic at St. Mary's Hospital.

seventy results in St. Mary's having the most even distribution of patients over the full range of age groups of any agency.

The predominance of younger adults among the patients using Westside agencies reflects the age distribution for the community. The most important development revealed by comparing data for 1968 and 1969/70 is the increase in numbers of older patients, especially people between the ages of forty and seventy. Much of this increase is accounted for by patients from this age range using the Crisis Clinic and the outpatient clinic at St. Mary's Hospital. The services offered by Westside following its establishment in 1969 appear to have been effective in reaching older individuals who previously had not sought therapeutic care.

Sex Distribution of Use

The sex distribution of patients first admitted to clinical services during the three sample months for 1969/70 shows that women outnumber men by 6 percent. This pattern of proportionate female dominance applies for all Westside outpatient services except the Crisis Clinic. The proportion of males using most of the outpatient facilities was higher for 1969/70 than for 1968. The exception was Cal. Med., where males accounted for 40.6 percent of the clients in 1968, but only 35.9 percent in 1969/70.

The client population of the Crisis Clinic is 52.8 percent male and 47.1 percent female for 1969/70. This service accounted for almost 10 percent more of all males using Westside outpatient services during this period than the comparable figures for females.

In summary, females use clinical psychiatric services in Westside more frequently than do males, but the proportionate use by these two groups is more equivalent for 1969/70 than is the case for 1968. This pattern applies for the agencies providing outpatient therapy, but not for the Crisis Clinic where men account for 5.7 percent more of the clients than do women. The Crisis Clinic provides short-term therapy, which appeals to the male population because, in general, they can less afford the time needed for intensive psychotherapy provided by the outpatient facilities. Further, Crisis Clinic services are available around the clock, whereas most outpatient clinics only treat patients during regular working hours.

Racial Distribution of Use

The racial distribution of Westside residents who were first admitted to clinics during the five sample months is 62.1 percent white, 31.1 percent black, 2.9 percent Mexican-American, and 1.8 percent Oriental and Filipino. Using 1960 population data for Westside, the percentage differences between the proportion of patients and population from each racial group reveal disparities in use among groups. Whites had a percentage difference of −3.9 percent, blacks 8.8 percent, and Mexican-Americans −1 percent.

Combination of Oriental and Filipino people with other racial groups in reported census data for tracts precludes an accurate computation for these. However, combining these patients with those for whom race was not recorded and subtracting the rate for population not included in the major racial categories gives a percentage difference of −3.9 percent. This is probably a conservative estimate of underutilization for these groups.

Use of private psychiatrists by some whites, especially those with high family incomes, may account for the relative underutilization of clinical services by this group. As evidence discussed in Chapter 3 suggests, the proportionate distribution of mental illness, especially among the lower-income black residents, probably substantially exceeds their proportionate representation among admissions to Westside agencies.

Mexican-Americans, along with Oriental and Filipino residents, are especially underrepresented among the people using Westside services. Very little is known concerning the reasons for their low rate of mental health service utilization. While members of these groups may be getting substitutes for psychiatric aid from institutions such as religious organizations,[5] an additional likely explanation for their relatively small numbers of users is lack of information about available care as well as cultural and social distance which inhibits their use. This is in part supported by the finding that Oriental and Filipino inpatients constitute 4.2 percent of the total first admissions to hospitalization during this five-month period. When individuals from these two groups use any Westside services, they are acutely disturbed and are usually directed rather than self-referred to mental health agencies.

A substantial problem, then, is identifying ways in which services should be provided to improve the mental health of these groups. A promising approach, adopted from an experimental program in New York City, would employ community workers from these populations to speak with individuals and at meetings to explain the nature and availability of these services.[6] This could be complemented by developing a special capability at one of the Westside agencies to provide meaningful and culturally compatable service for members of these various groups. These methods would be equally appropriate for improving the psychological accessibility to services for poor black residents of the area.

Income Distribution of Use

While family income is a valuable demographic variable for analyzing the use of publicly subsidized clinical mental health services, recording practices of the various agencies cause the data to be of little worth. Of agencies receiving Short-Doyle funds, 23 percent of the patients admitted to the Crisis Clinic had no recorded income, and blanks appeared for from 46 percent to 80 percent of the patients admitted at other agencies. Staff at some agencies explained that the question concerning the income on admission forms was disregarded on principle or to avoid discouraging the client from seeking therapy. Clearly, data with such high proportions of missing observations can be of little assistance in analyzing the use of clinical mental health services.

Cal. Med., which receives no reimbursement for patients from Short-Doyle funds, provided the only complete information on family incomes. Only 23.5 percent of the 200 patients admitted by this agency over the five sample months exceeded the Short-Doyle maximum gross monthly family income of $720. The median income for these patients is between $500 and $582. The range of incomes is from less than $167 (3.5 percent) to $917 or greater (10 percent). As expected, the distribution is skewed toward the higher incomes, but the mode falls between $334 and $582 per month.

The Crisis Clinic, providing the most complete data of all the remaining agencies, has a median family income of less than $167. Of the 55 percent of all patients to Westside agencies for whom incomes are reported, the median monthly gross family income is also the lowest extreme, less than $167. While the data are very incomplete, it appears that clients of Westside's services are predominately individuals who are widely considered to be the poor or working poor.

Distribution of Patients by Diagnosis

Diagnostic categories provide a basis for examining the types of psychiatric problems affecting a group of patients. Mental health professionals evaluate and record the mental condition of patients both at the time of admission to a Westside agency and and at the time of referral or discharge. Diagnoses used in this analysis are defined in Chapter 3.

We are primarily interested in examining the proportionate distribution of various demographic groups of patients by diagnostic categories to identify especially prevalent types of problems. This analysis is of value both in seeking to identify and explain differences in mental health between groups and in designing service delivery systems which respond to the psychiatric needs of these groups. This part of the investigation focuses on black and white clients because the numbers from other racial groups are proportionately very small, and on adults between the ages of sixteen and fifty to control for mental problems unique or most frequent with the young and old.

The most frequent diagnosis for all Westside outpatients and for both black (27.8 percent) and white (41.5 percent) clients for 1968 is for personality disorders. Neuroses emerges as the predominant reported condition for all admissions during the three months representing 1969/70. However, the proportionate distribution of patients by diagnosis shows a marked difference when black and white clients are analyzed separately. While neurosis is the most prevalent condition for white patients (N = 634) during 1969/70, psychosis (22.4 percent) and personality disorder (24.2 percent) are proportionately nearly as important diagnostic categories.[c] These three conditions account for 75.8 percent of the white clients.

In contrast, the most prevalent diagnosis for black patients (N = 223) during 1969/70 is drug addiction (27.8 percent), followed in importance by psychosis (26.8 percent) and neurosis (20.6 percent), with personality disorders (9.4 percent) accounting for only about one-third of the 1968 rate. Black patients increased by a factor of about twelve between 1968 and 1969/70, and the effects of this change include a 4-fold increase in patients diagnosed as having personality disorders, while neurotic patients increased about 12-fold, and psychotic 30-fold. Thus increasing numbers of patients and institution of services for drug addicts are largely responsible for the changes in the proportionate distribution of black patients by diagnostic category.

Of the Mexican-American clients in 1969/70, 34.6 percent (9) are diagnosed as drug addicted, while psychotic and neurotic categories each account for 23.1 percent (6) of these patients. Of Oriental patients, 44.4 percent (4) are diagnosed as psychotic.

Assessment of diagnoses for clients from residential areas, as defined in Chapter 6, provides information concerning the spatial distribution of mental health problems as currently evaluated and treated at Westside agencies. Psychosis (N = 267) is a highly frequent diagnosis only for patients from Alamo (13.9 percent) and the Haight (14.9 percent). High proportions of drug addicted clients (N = 124) come from Western Addition North (19.4 percent) and South (21.8 percent), Alamo (22.6 percent), and the Haight (17.7 percent).

Outpatients with neurosis (N = 318) most frequently come from Alamo (8.8 percent) and the Haight (9.1 percent), but these proportions are not as great as for psychosis. These two areas also have the highest proportions of patients with diagnosis of gross stress and adjustment reaction. The Marina, Pacific Heights, and Buena Vista have slightly higher proportions of patients diagnosed as having personality disorders than do the other areas.

The largest proportions of patients with organic brain disease (N = 23) come from the Haight (21.7 percent) and Buena Vista (13 percent), followed by Western Addition North (8.7 percent). Although this condition may be associated with high drug use, comparison with areas having high proportions of drug-addicted patients shows little correlation. While Haight and Western

---

[c]The white dominance of personality disorders as a category suggests that this could be a convenient and polite diagnosis which may have been applied inequitably among races.

Addition North have relatively high numbers of addicted patients, Buena Vista does not. Further, Western Addition South and Alamo, which have high proportions of addicted patients do not have high proportions of organic brain disease patients.

In summary, Haight, Alamo, and Western Addition North and South followed by Buena Vista, have the highest proportions of patients for several diagnostic categories in addition to high total proportionate use of Westside services. To the extent that patients and diagnoses represent the mental health conditions of resident populations, these findings point up areas with special mental health problems. Even though caution should be used in making such an inference, this information does suggest where efforts to increase the availability of mental health service might be focused.

Withdrawal from Therapy

The rates at which patients complete rather than withdraw from therapy provides one indicator of the extent to which clinical services provided by Westside are satisfactory from the perspective of current users. This is of course not an unambiguous measure of acceptability, since withdrawal may be a function of an individual's situation and unrelated to the satisfaction realized from the psychiatric service received and the manner in which it is provided.

The final disposition of cases is noted on patients' records. This data was classified as to whether the patient withdrew from service against medical advice, or did not withdraw but either completed therapy and was discharged by the therapist or was referred to another agency for additional care. For the three months representing 1969/70 for which data was collected, 63.5 percent of all patients using the several Westside agencies completed therapy or were referred. The rates for patients who did not withdraw from therapy vary by agency from the high for Mt. Zion (71) percent to the lowest (37.8 percent) for the clinic at PMC. The rate of completion for St. Mary's is 66.4 percent, for the Crisis Clinic is 64.4 percent, and for Children's is 59.4 percent. Data on this item was not available from Cal. Med.

It is difficult to establish what constitutes a desirable or acceptable completion rate, for some of the reasons suggested concerning problems with using withdrawals versus discharges as a measure of adequacy for the service. An approach to this issue involves tentatively accepting the best performance by any agency as a criterion. Using Mt. Zion's 71 percent rate of completion, most of the other agencies come within about ten points of achieving an equal performance. Viewed in terms of withdrawals which reduce the effectiveness of the therapy received, these centers have dropout rates of between 34 and 41 percent, with the most extreme case losing 62 percent of its patients to withdrawals. These figures do appear to be excessive, especially for outpatient centers providing therapeutic programs intended to have long-term effects in contrast to the Crisis Clinic service for providing short-term assistance. In other words, while most clinics appear from these data to satisfy a majority of their patients, current performance is not acceptable and efforts should be made to reduce dropouts to more nearly 25 percent of all patients entering therapy.

A related but less powerful indicator of the satisfaction received from outpatient services is the proportion of patients by diagnostic category who seek service and actually enter therapy. Because the first two or three interview sessions with a newly admitted patient are largely concerned with history and diagnosis, the criterion used is those patients continuing for four or more sessions. The Crisis Clinic had large numbers of patients but few who met this criterion since many use this service for very short-term assistance. For this reason and to reduce bias in the analysis, data for this agency was omitted.

Proportions of patients first admitted to the five Westside outpatient clinics during the three months representing 1969/70 and remaining in therapy for four or more sessions ranged from 54.2 percent for those with a diagnosis of transient situational disturbances to 25.8 percent for psychotic patients. Other categories with highfrequencies of patients include psychoneurotic with 42.5 percent of the patients completing four or more sessions, and personality disorders with 38.9 percent.

The criterion used in this analysis appears to be minimal and perhaps too low, especially for complicated psychiatric conditions such as psychosis and neurosis. Yet only a quarter to two-fifths of the admitted patients from these categories continued therapy through four sessions. To the extent that this measure is a realistic indicator of the satisfaction of patients and the therapeutic adequacy of the amount of service consumed, Westside Center outpatient clinics appear to perform at a lower level than suggested by the previous indicator.

Sources of Referral to Clinical Mental Health Services

How various groups of patients gain access to the mental health care delivery system is useful for identifying which agents should be major clients in designing an information program to facilitate the use of psychiatric services. Sources of referral also reveal where people who sooner or later use clinical services tend to take their emotional problems. Finally, this information allows an assessment of the role played by referrals in the choice of the agency at which service is sought.

The source of referral was recorded for patients using Westside Center agencies as part of the admissions procedure. Investigation of how patients entered mental health care was accomplished by aggregating fifty-seven sources of referral into five classes, referral by self or family, from a medical service such as a hospital, by a physician, by a social service agent or agency, and a residual category for other sources. Analysis of 431 observations, the first admissions from October 1969, involved disaggregating the group of patients from each of these sources by race and by diagnostic class (Table 6-1).

Our interest is in identifying different patterns of referral by patients of various racial groups, standardizing, standardizing for psychiatric condition. Patterns of referral into service are found to differ markedly by diagnosis, as do proportionate distributions of patients by race. Social service agencies and physicians are less prevalent sources of referral than expected. Proportions of patients coming from each source are calculated by race and diagnosis so that the relative importance of sources may be compared.[d]

Among sources of referrals, self-referred dominates in all diagnostic categories except transient situational disturbances in which social agencies are the largest referral group. Small numbers make this latter finding difficult to interpret meaningfully, but students referred by school counselors appear to be a major source of these patients. Physicians are also important referral agents for white patients with this diagnosis.

Social service agencies, especially social workers and police, are unusually frequent sources of referral for both black and white patients diagnosed as psychotic. Acutely deviant behavior, which is commonly related with this diagnostic category, apparently encourages resort to social agents for assistance in getting the psychotic individual into treatment.[e]

Patients diagnosed as drug addicted are almost entirely self-referred. This reflects the nature of the program for this group, which is fully voluntary and primarily provides direction for people seeking detoxification.

A major referral difference between clients by race in the several diagnostic groups is the important role played by medical services in the admission of black and Mexican-American consumers of outpatient care. Referral by medical services is almost twice as important for black than for white psychotic patients, and almost four times as important for black psychoneurotic patients. Hospital clinics are the most common source of medical assistance for low-income black families. These clinics appear to be used, out of habit, in seeking referral, and also commonly identify psychiatric conditions meriting attention among clients with other complaints.

Because of these patterns, a close working relationship between the

---

[d]When Table 6-1 is disaggregated into a series of tabulations differentiated by diagnosis, the lambda coefficient of nominal correlation for most of the resulting tables is less than 0.05. Only in the subtable for transient situational diagnosis does the lambda suggest that race influences source of referral ($\lambda = 0.10$). The lambda calculated on the basis of subtotals of the aggregated table (0.115) suggest that there is a relationship between diagnosis and race, that is that knowing the diagnosis slightly improves the prediction of the race of a patient. For a discussion of Goodman-Kruskal's lambda, see footnote [a] of this chapter. Data on referrals to private psychiatrists was not available.

[e]Police will respond to client calls for a ride to the Crisis Clinic, or to a neighbor's calls to pick someone up, however most of these individuals are recorded as self referred.

Table 6-1

Source of Referral to Therapy by Diagnosis and Race for Patients First Admitted during October, 1969[a]

Diagnosis; Source of Referral	Racial Groups			
	Caucasian %	Black %	Mexican-American %	Oriental %
Psychotic:				
Self-Referred	36.5	42.4	-	-
Medical Services	9.5	18.2	100.0	-
Private Physician	-	3.0	-	-
Soc. Service Agency	21.6	15.2	-	100.0
Other	32.4	21.2	-	-
Total	100.0 (N = 74)	100.0 (N = 33)	100.0 (N = 2)	100.0 (N = 2)
Neurotic:				
Self-Referred	56.3	55.2	50.0	-
Medical Services	4.6	17.2	25.0	-
Private Physician	6.9	6.9	-	-
Soc. Service Agency	5.8	3.5	-	-
Total	100.0 (N = 87)	100.0 (N = 29)	100.0 (N = 4)	-
Personality Disorder:				
Self Referred	44.3	50.0	-	-
Medical Services	1.6	50.0	-	-
Private Physician	4.9	-	-	-
Soc. Service Agency	13.1	-	-	100.0
Other	36.1	-	-	-
Total	100.0 (N = 61)	100.0 (N = 2)	-	100.0 (N = 1)
Drug Addiction:				
Self-Referred	86.8	93.6	83.3	-
Medical Services	-	3.2	-	-
Private Physician	-	-	-	-
Soc. Service Agency	6.1	-	16.7	-
Other	6.1	3.2	-	-
Total	100.0 (N = 15)	100.0 (N = 31)	100.0 (N = 6)	-
Transient Situational:				
Self-Referred	13.6	11.1	-	-
Medical Services	13.6	-	-	-
Private Physician	18.3	-	-	-
Soc. Service Agency	31.8	66.7	-	-
Other	22.7	22.2	100.0	100.0
Total	100.0 (N = 22)	100.0 (N = 9)	100.0 (N = 1)	100.0 (N = 1)

Table 6-1 continued

| Diagnosis; Source of Referral | Racial Groups | | | |
	Caucasian %	Black %	Mexican-American %	Oriental %
All Other Diagnosis:				
Self-Referred	58.3	33.3	-	-
Medical Services	4.2	-	-	-
Private Physician	4.2	-	-	-
Soc. Service Agency	20.8	-	-	-
Other	12.5	66.7	-	-
Total	100.0	100.0	-	-
	(N = 24)	(N = 3)	-	-

[a]Missing data on diagnosis or race required that twenty-four observations be omitted from this table.

community mental health center and hospital medical clinics could improve the ease of referral and admission of low-income people with mental health problems to appropriate psychiatric services. The hospitals could provide a more extensive screening and interpretive service, and recommendations from this source tend to be heeded more readily than nonmedical advice.

The data of course deal only with current patterns of behavior. While social service agencies are of limited importance as sources of referral, this may result in part from poor information available to agency workers concerning situtations in which therapy could be appropriate, and concerning how and where such therapy could be obtained. A carefully designed program of consultation and information for workers in each group of social agencies, from pastors to police, could increase their effectiveness as sources of referral.

The value resulting from counseling programs for social and medical agents could take several forms. In addition to generally disseminating information, these agents could identify those of their clients who appear to need help with emotional problems and advise these people concerning where these services may be obtained. With a modest amount of training, these agents could themselves assist clients with many of their emotional problems.

Whether these agents provided direct assistance or referred clients to Westside agencies, information and close working relationships would facilitate early treatment of emotional disturbances before they became more complex psychiatric problems. Similarly, counseling could inform social agents of appropriate alternatives to mental health services, for example, of agencies especially able to deal with functional issues or special problems that are the source of abnormal and destructive stress. Referral of clients to the most appropriate agency or service group would not only be the most effective service from the client's perspective, but would also increase the effectiveness with which differing, special purpose services are used.

Finally, the role of self-referral as the major current method of entry into mental health care suggests the importance of public information. Efforts to increase the awareness and acceptance of clinical services to various groups in the population of the catchment should seek to identify media which are most effective in reaching and influencing these groups. For example, while groups with relatively high levels of education may respond to written information, groups with little education appear to most readily accept verbally communicated information. For the latter, indigenous community workers who have reliable information concerning the availability and nature of therapeutic services could be effective in increasing the awareness of this public and even in directly helping individuals to use the program.[7]

The distribution of patients admitted during October 1969 among Westside agencies (Table 6-2) again demonstrates the importance of self-referral as a major means of entering care. As expected, a large majority (70 percent) of the people using the short-term, walk-in service at the Crisis Clinic are self-referred. Referrals grouped and shown as other sources most frequently come from private psychiatrists.

Social service agencies appear as especially important referral sources for patients using Mt. Zion and Pacific Medical Center, and as relatively important in the case of St. Mary's. Welfare workers and school counselors were the major referral agents within this grouping. This pattern may result from exceptional information which these agents currently have concerning the appropriateness of services available at these clinics for their clients.

Private physicians account for relatively fewer referrals than expected, when compared with aggregates of other sources. Examining specific sources other than self-referral, physicians rank fourth in importance behind social work agencies, general hospitals, and private psychiatrists in the frequency of patients using this route of referral. In other words, doctors in private practice are an important specific source of referral, but are secondary to sources serving predominately poorer people and to independent psychiatrists serving primarily people with high incomes.[f]

The unusually important role played by medical services as a source of referral to Children's Hospital further supports the hypothesis that the recently instituted outpatient services for adults at this agency is not widely popularly known. The relative unimportance of social service agencies in referrals to Children's Hospital is probably similarly the result of a lack of information on their part.

---

[f]Private doctors refer a relatively large proportion of white patients (5 percent) to mental health services. When medical services and private physicians as grouped sources of referral are combined, they account for somewhat more comparable proportions of referral across races; 11 percent for whites, 13 percent for blacks, 16.7 percent for Mexican-Americans, and 25 percent for Oriental patients.

Table 6-2

Sources of Referral to Westside Agencies for Patients Admitted During October, 1969

Source of Referral	Agency						Total
	Cal. Med.	Children's	Crisis Clinic	Mt. Zion	PMC	St. Mary's	
Self-Referral	17 (37.0)	6 (40.0)	139 (70.0)	10 (16.4)	4 (20.0)	28 (31.1)	204 (47.3)
Medical Services	3 (6.5)	3 (20.0)	23 (11.5)	1 (1.6)	0	2 (2.2)	32 (7.4)
Private Physicians	3 (6.5)	1 (6.7)	2 (1.0)	2 (3.3)	0	9 (10.0)	17 (4.0)
Soc. Service Agencies	4 (8.7)	1 (6.7)	20 (10.0)	11 (18.0)	5 (25.0)	19 (21.1)	60 (13.9)
Other Sources	19 (41.3)	4 (26.6)	15 (7.5)	37 (60.7)	11 (55.0)	32 (35.6)	118 (27.4)
Total Patients	46 (100.%)	15 (100.%)	199 (100.%)	61 (100.%)	20 (100.%)	90 (100.%)	431 (100.%)

The lambda coefficient of association for agencies, given source of referral, is 0.397. This suggests that referrals, including personal choice, play a substantial role in the differential use of agencies offering clinical care, and the consequent importance of information in influencing not only the use of various agencies but the magnitude of use of mental health services.

Summary and Conclusions

Demographic profiles of people using outpatient services and of the residential population provide a basis for identifying groups which are underrepresented among current clients, and for modifying the service delivery system to accomodate all groups more successfully. Young adults are the predominant age group using outpatient services provided by Westside Center member agencies. While this reflects the age composition of the catchment population, the elderly appear to be underrepresented among those currently using services. Clients are more frequently female than male, except at the Crisis Clinic, but the proportions recently have become more equivalent.

Caucasions use outpatient services about 4 percent less and Mexican-Americans 1 percent less than expected on the basis of their contribution to the population, while black clients are almost 9 percent more frequent than expected on this basis. Purchase of these services from the private sector by the first of these groups probably explains their use of subsidized care. More extensive employment of indigenous paraprofessionals and development of local centers with special capabilities and programs are promising means of making outpatient services more attractive and useful to poorer residents of the area. Differences in the importance of various diagnoses among the several client groups, by race and by residential location, further suggest the desirability of these policy proposals.

The rate of withdrawal from therapy at most clinics appears to be excessively high and indicates the desirability of improving the attractiveness of the service packages provided at these clinics.

Information on sources of referral is important in determining how people seek and obtain therapy, and in designing information programs for referral agents and consumer groups. Social service agencies and physicians were less frequently cited as sources of referral than had been expected, suggesting the desirability of a program to make them more aware of mental health problems and where services may be obtained. Many black and Mexican-American clients are referred by medical services such as hospital clinics. This seems to indicate that psychiatric problems are often viewed as medical problems by members of these groups. These clinics might be further developed as sources of information, and collaborative arrangements made to facilitate direct referrals to agencies and perhaps to specific therapists. The dominant importance of self-rerral indicates the value of identifying the media which is most effective in reaching and influencing various groups of consumers and in providing usuable and reliable information by these means concerning when help would be appropriate and where it may be secured.

7

The Influence of Physical Accessibility on Utilization of Clinical Services Provided by Westside Mental Health Center

Much of the previous health services research dealing with consumer demand behavior has concentrated on physical accessibility, as was pointed out in Chapter 2. In this chapter, we pursue a user-oriented approach to analysis in seeking to determine the most desirable spatial distribution of clinical mental health services which act as collection points for clients. Rather than simply trying to identify a set of locations which would minimize the aggregate distance traveled by current patients, or more appropriately the entire population to be served by several agencies or facilities, we first investigate the effect of physical distance on current patients.

If increasing distance, within the confines of the Westside Mental Health District or catchment, appears to have little effect on the rates of utilization standardized for the distribution of population, then the locational question may be of little consequence in this context. Of additional importance from a user-oriented perspective is the differential effect of distance or its inverse, accessibility, on various consumer groups. Does distance, for example, appear to have little effect on the Mexican-American clients, and a substantial effect on Caucasian users? Does an increase in distance affect the relative frequency with which patients with various diagnoses fully enter therapy? Does the distance which must be traveled to a clinic appear to influence premature withdrawal from treatment? And as an extension of our analysis dealing with the effect of different types of service for ambulatory patients on user choice and consumption, do people travel further for some of these services than for others?

These are the questions which we seek to answer in this chapter. This information will begin to suggest components and relations of a consumer-demand function for public mental health services. This information will also raise further questions such as the extent to which information could be substituted for accessibility to result in the same level of demand for a given population. Some of these questions cannot be resolved with the available data.

The Influence of Distance on General Client Demand Behavior for Clinical Mental Health Services

The effect of distance on use of clinical mental health services may be assessed by examining the relative frequency with which patients travel various distances between their place of residence and clinics in order to receive therapy. Our

93

measure of revealed demand is the number of patients first admitted to agencies during several sample months.

For purposes of this analysis, distances which clients traveled to secure service are classified by a series of five distance zones. These zones consist of census tracts, which are allocated to one of the five zones on the basis of the distance between the centroid of the tract and each of the six Westside Center Agencies currently providing clinical services.[a] Thus each agency is surrounded by a comparable system of five concentric distance zones.

Numbers of patients using each agency are then standardized for differences in the population sizes of the census tracts constituting the concentric distance zones relating to that agency. Standardization was accomplished by linearly transforming the population number for each zone for each center into a set of relative weights which were then applied to the frequencies of patients using each center by their distance zone of origin.[b]

Analysis of the resulting transformed data permits assessing the effect of distance on utilization of these services in a manner which accounts for distance at a set of intervals which are comparable for all clinical centers, facilitates accounting for racial differences in the population, and accounts for differences in the size of these populations. The extent to which variations in utilization are not accounted for by distance then points up what must be explained by other variables such as differences in the services provided by the several mental health agencies and available to residents of the catchment.

Table 7-1 presents the relative frequencies of all patients, at each of the six Westside Center agencies, from each of the five distance zones concentric to the respective agency. These proportions were computed from frequencies of patients first admitted during the three sample months representing 1969/70, standardized for zonal population sizes.

Inspection of this table reveals that no pattern for all clinical agencies or strong trend over distance zones for any particular agency emerges, with one exception. The Crisis Clinic shows not only a relatively consistent proportionate

---

[a]These distances have been adjusted to account both for actual street distances between locations and for the pattern of public transportation service in the Westside District. Consequently, the comparable zones for the six agencies represent estimated isoquant maps of time-distances.

Because census tracts are assigned to zones on the basis of distance, the relative distribution of population by zones for a particular agency demonstrates the extent to which that agency is centrally located to the residential distribution of people living in the Westside District.

[b]A reverse weighting scale was constructed by assigning the smallest zonal population a base index, for example the number ten, expressing the next smallest zonal population as a fraction of the smallest, etc. For example, $6,452/7,624 = 0.85$, $0.85 \times 10 = 8.5$; $6,452/8,267 = 0.78$, $0.78 \times 10 = 7.8$, etc. The resulting weights are applied to actual frequency figures to account for the greater importance of a given number of clients from a smaller population at risk than from a larger zonal population. Tables based on frequencies standardized for variations in population sizes of analysis areas are noted as such. Values for standardized and unstandardized variables are usually not equivalent.

Table 7-1

Distribution of All Westside Patients Residing in the District, By Distance, for Clinical Service Agencies, First Admissions for Three Months, 1969-1970

	Clinic Used					
Distance Zone	Cal. Med. %	Children's %	Crisis Clinic %	Mt. Zion %	PMC %	St. Mary's %
1.	46.8	23.3	20.4	38.4	17.4	60.3
2.	22.0	22.1	11.8	15.7	8.3	21.4
3.	3.7	30.2	19.5	9.4	48.8	7.1
4.	6.4	7.0	21.1	28.3	16.5	3.8
5.	21.1	17.4	27.1	8.2	9.0	7.4
Total	100.0	100.0	100.0	100.0	100.0	100.0
	(N = 109)[a]	(N = 86)	(N = 845)	(N = 159)	(N = 121)	(N = 365)

[a]Frequencies standardized for variations in population sizes of distance zones.

distribution of patients over the full range of distance zones analyzed, but also some increase in proportionate use with increasing distance. The interpretation of this phenomenon is that the Crisis Clinic, offering a unique type of service to Westside District residents, attracts those clients who favor this short-term form of therapy, regardless of their residential location. Additionally, we can infer that the boundaries of the district are well within the spatial range of the services supplied by the Crisis Clinic.

The conventional outpatient center which most closely approximates the relative spatial distribution of clients observed for the Crisis Clinic is Children's Hospital. While the attenuating effect of distance on patient trips is apparent, there is a more nearly equal distribution of clients with distance than for any of the other centers. Children's Hospital is also exceptional in that it had only 5.1 percent of the first admissions to the six clinical centers for the three months representing 1969/70. It appears that this little known agency provides uncrowded, desirable service for those few who have information about its availability.

California Psychiatric, Mt. Zion, and St. Mary's clearly demonstrate the attenuating effect of distance on general use over the first three distance zones, while each of the first two then receive about a quarter of their clients from the fourth or fifth zones. Differing from these, the modal number of clients for Pacific Presbyterian comes from distance zone three.

As expected with this variety of client distributions with distance, the lambda coefficient of correlation dealing with the influence of distance on choice of agency is very close to zero (0.056). The dominance of the Crisis Clinic, as the agency of first admission for almost 40 percent of the clients for the three-month period, and its somewhat constant distribution of standardized relative frequencies of patients over distance, appears to largely determine this result. Analyzing the five outpatient centers exclusive of the Crisis Clinic gives a lambda of 0.135, suggesting that distance does have a modest influence on the choice of clinic for patients viewed as a single population.[c]

The Influence of Distance on Use of Types of Clinical Service

Analysis of the patient distribution by distance zone for various clinical agencies revealed a difference between the spatial use of the Crisis Clinic and conventional outpatient services. This difference is brought into focus when all outpatient clinics are combined and data on use with distance is contrasted with comparable data for the Crisis Clinic. Table 7-2 demonstrates that while relative use of the outpatient facilities monotonically decreases with increasing distance, proportionate use of the Crisis Clinic monotonically increases.[d] The greatest percentage difference for each of these two types of centers is between zones two and three.

The proportionate distributions of patients over zones reveals that while the effect of distance on use of all outpatient centers takes the well-known negative exponential form, proportionate use of the Crisis Clinic generally increases with distance. With the exception of the proportion coming from zone two (Table 7-1), the relative frequency curve for patients using the Crisis Clinic would be almost linear with a slight positive slope.

In other words, while distance has the conventional result of attenuating the relative frequency of trip-making to outpatient centers, when viewed as a group, use of the Crises Clinic seems to be unaffected by distance. Thus demand for this service is virtually inelastic with respect to distance. It appears that for many clients, the expected value of service available at the Crisis Clinic exceeds that available from closer outpatient centers, offsetting the increased cost of trip-making.

It is important to remember that these data are for current patients, who are expected to resemble but not totally represent those individuals who continue to constitute latent demand for mental health services. These data do suggest that it is more practical to centralize the provision of short-term therapy than conventional long-term therapy. However, it appears that some decentralization of services of the type provided by the Crisis Clinic would increase effective demand by increasing the net benefit to current nonusers to a level which would encourage them to make use of the service.

---

[c]Lambdas for rows, given columns, are 0.088 in the first case, and 0.059 in the second. See footnote [a] in Chapter 6 for a discussion of the lambda.

[d]The lambda for columns as the dependent variable is 0.305, suggesting that distance accounts for about 30 percent of the variation in the use of the two types of service.

Table 7-2

Distribution of Patients by Type of Service for Distance Zones, First Admissions for Three Months, 1969/70.

Distance Zones	Type of Service		
	Outpatient Centers %	Crisis Clinic %	Total %
1.	70.2	31.8	100.0 (N = 546)[a]
2.	61.0	39.0	100.0 (N = 256)
3.	44.0	56.0	100.0 (N = 295)
4.	34.0	66.0	100.0 (N = 270)
5.	28.0	72.0	100.0 (N = 318)

[a]Frequencies standardized for variations in population sizes of distance zones.

The Influence of Distance on Premature Withdrawal from Therapy

Another approach to analyzing the influence of distance on consumer behavior is to compare the relative frequencies of patients withdrawing from therapy with those being discharged or referred to another service. The hypothesis is that with increasing distances, the rate of withdrawal will increase relative to the rate of completion and discharge. A pattern of this sort would suggest that greater distances result in larger costs to the consumer and will consequently lead to a disproportionate number of patients prematurely discontinuing therapy. A remedial policy could aim toward decreasing patient costs in securing therapy by spatially decentralizing the availability of services, thus encouraging patients to complete therapy.

This analysis reveals that withdrawals against medical advice are more frequent than discharges and referrals at most agencies for the outermost concentric distance zones centered on these agencies. This is the case for two of the three most distant zones for Children's Hospital and Pacific Presbyterian, and for the three most distant zones for Mt. Zion. St. Mary's Hospital is the major exception among conventional outpatient clinics, with large relative percentages of patients who come from distant zones and complete therapy. The Crisis Clinic shows no particular pattern.

The hypothesis appears to be confirmed by the proportional dominance of withdrawals over discharges for the three most distant zones, especially for outpatient centers. However, the hypothesis also suggests that discharges should proportionately exceed withdrawals for zones closer to the center supplying therapeutic care. This is less clearly the case. The proportion of patients discharged exceeds the proportion who withdrew in only one of the two closest zones for each of the outpatient centers. Two of these centers and the Crisis Clinic do, however, have essentially equal rates for premature termination and discharge for one of these zones each. Thus, while comparative rates for nearby zones do not strongly support the hypothesis, neither do they refute it.

The difference in the consumer behavior of patients using the Crisis Clinic and conventional outpatient services suggests the desirability of comparing these as two categories of therapeutic care. Assessing pairs of columns by type of service in Table 7-3, discharges are found to be proportionately equal or slightly less than withdrawals for patients using conventional outpatient centers and coming from the three most remote distance zones with reference to the center used. Of the closer zones, the proportion of discharges for zone two was about twice that for withdrawals, while zone one had high proportions of both discharges and withdrawals.[e]

In marked contrast, the proportionate distribution of discharges and referrals from the Crisis Clinic is skewed toward the most distant zones. As a consequence, relative frequencies of discharges exceed those for withdrawal by about ten points for zones three and four and are roughly equivalent for zone five. Discharges are not as proportionately frequent as expected for the two closest zones. In other words, the hypothesis that premature withdrawals will increase relative to discharges with increases in distance appears to apply for outpatient center; however, it does not apply for the Crisis Clinic.

The Crisis Clinic, which offers only emergency and short-term therapy, is currently the primary source of the former and the only source of the latter service for residents of the Westside District. Differences in the spatial distribution of discharges and referrals do not stem from a higher rate of discharges connected with short-term therapy. Discharges and referrals account for about 65 percent of the patients from each type of service for whom data on case disposition was available. Some referrals from the Crisis Clinic to other agencies may be from the more distant zones to psychiatric services more accessible to the client.

More importantly, the difference seen in consumer behavior with respect to these two types of service is probably explained by the attractiveness of the services available only at the Crisis Clinic and the consequent willingness of

---

[e]The lambda for discharges with zones as the independent variable is 0.193; that distance accounts for about one-fifth of the variation in absolute standardized frequencies of discharges for the two types of agency.

Table 7-3

Distance Distribution of Patients Withdrawing and Completing Therapy by Type
of Service, for Patients First Admitted During Three Sample Months, 1969/70

| Distance Zones | Nature of Termination and Type of Service | | | |
| | Withdrawals | | Discharges and Referrals | |
	Outpatient Clinics %	Crisis Clinic %	Outpatient Clinics %	Crisis Clinic %
1.	44.3	38.0	32.8	16.0
2.	9.1	13.8	22.6	13.3
3.	16.7	21.4	15.6	31.0
4.	13.3	9.9	13.3	22.4
5.	15.8	16.8	16.0	17.2
Total	100.0 (N = 119)[a]	100.0 (N = 131)	100.0 (N = 225)	100.0 (N = 187)

[a]Frequencies standardized for variations in population sizes of distance zones.

many clients to incur the greater trip-making costs to reach this center. This
constitutes a measure of demand for these services and suggests that increased
frequency of use by residents, including currently latent demand, would result
from provision of these services at several locations.

Thus, rather than interpreting the above findings as supporting continued
centralization of services now supplied by the Crisis Clinic and further
decentralizing centers supplying conventional therapeutic care, a different
conclusion is suggested. Greater dispersal of both types of services, thus
decreasing the distance which must currently be traveled to reach supplying
agencies, should increase the relative proportions of clients completing their
therapeutic programs.

The Influence of Distance on Behavior of Clients from Various Racial Groups

In light of the preceeding findings concerning the effect of distance on aggregate
consumer behavior, it would be expected that use of clinical services by patients,
disaggregated by racial group membership, would decline with distance. This is
not consistently the case for the 1969/70 sample months; the distribution of
patients for the three major racial groups by distance zones varies widely.

The modal frequency for white patients (47 percent) falls in zone one and is
followed by a relatively consistent decline with distance. Similarly, the greatest
frequency for Mexican-Americans come from zone one (31.8 percent), but a
high frequency of patients from zone three (24.8 percent) gives this distribution

a second mode. The distribution for black patients is also bimodal, but at the extremes. These three differing distributions result in a lambda for influence of distance on racial composition of the patient population of only 0.157.

Differences in the effect of distance on clients by racial group are more pronounced when separate relative frequency distributions for outpatient centers (Table 7-4) and the Crisis Clinic (Table 7-5) are examined. Each of the racial groups show a decline in the relative frequency of people using outpatient centers as zones become more distant. These declines are especially marked after the first zone for whites, the second for blacks, and the third for Mexican-

Table 7-4

Patients Using Outpatient Centers by Race and Distance, First Admissions for Three Sample Months, 1969/1970

Distance Zone	Race of Patient		
	Caucasian %	Black %	Mexican-American %
1.	42.9	38.3	59.5
2.	15.1	31.4	-
3.	14.2	10.4	28.0
4.	12.1	9.0	12.5
5.	15.7	10.8	-
Total	100.0 (N = 338)[a]	100.0 (N = 334)	100.0 (N = 168)

[a]Frenquencies standardized for variations in population sizes of distance zones.

Table 7-5

Patients Using Crisis Clinic by Race and Distance, First Admissions for Three Sample Months, 1969/1970

Distance Zone	Race of Patient		
	Caucasian %	Black %	Mexican-American %
1.	52.0	5.2	-
2.	10.2	7.9	26.0
3.	18.4	19.7	21.2
4.	10.2	31.3	14.4
5.	9.2	35.9	38.4
Total	100.0 (N = 293)[a]	100.0 (N = 406)	100.0 (N = 146)

[a]Frequencies standardized for variations in population sizes of distance zones.

Americans. However, the lambda denoting the influence of distance on the frequencies of patients by race is only 0.108.

In contrast, Table 7-5 for the Crisis Clinic demonstrates that proportions of patients by race, standardized for population, tend to increase with distance. The exception is the distribution for white patients, which shows a relatively consistent decline in use with increasing distances. Blacks and Mexican-Americans show increases in use over distance zones three, four and five, often at a magnitude of around 10 percent of the total patients from that race. Here, the lambdas are a relatively high 0.253 for the influence of distance on frequencies of people by race using the Crisis Clinic, and 0.203 for the improvement in predicting distance given race.

Plots of these data show that whites use both types of service at declining frequencies with distance in a manner closely related to conventional distance decay curves. Black patients, on the other hand, use outpatient clinics more frequently at nearby locations and less frequently at greater distances than do whites. A reversal of behavior, increasing use with distance, occurs in the case of the Crisis Clinic. The curve is almost linear and has a positive slope of about one.

The direction of the influence of distance on the consumption behavior of Mexican-Americans is similar, though less consistent, to that for black patients. Use of outpatient clinics declines with distance, but fluctuates from zero to a figure proportionately greater than for other races in zone three. Use of the Crisis Clinic roughly parallels the curve for black patients, but fluctuates from a higher relative value for zone two to a lower value for zone four.

Further disaggregation of this data for patients by race and distance zone, but accounting additionally for differences in the use of various outpatient centers, yields little additional information concerning the influence of distance on use. This data is used in the next chapter, however, to analyze the differential use of various outpatient centers by racial groups.

The Influence of Distance on the Behavior of Clients with Vairious Diagnoses

In addition to racial group membership, diagnosis or the nature of the presented problems is a characteristic of clients which may affect their sensitivity to distance in consuming mental health services. For purposes of analyzing the differences in behavior of patients by diagnosis, we have used data on clients who have completed four or more interview sessions and thus have finished the intake process and have entered therapy.

Table 7-6 presents the proportion of patients, by diagnosis and type of service consumed, for each of the five distance zones. Frequencies are for patients first admitted during the three sample months for 1969/70 and are standardized for the population sizes of the various distance zones. The hypostheses are that the

Table 7-6

Patients Attending Four of More Therapy Sessions, by Diagnosis, Type of Service Used, and Distance, First Admissions for Three Sample Months, 1969/1970

Diagnosis and Type of Service

Distance Zone	Psychotic O.P. %	Psychotic Crisis Clinic %	Neurotic O.P. %	Neurotic Crisis Clinic %	Personality Disorders O.P. %	Personality Disorders Crisis Clinic %	Drug Addiction O.P. %	Drug Addiction Crisis Clinic %
1.	39.6	-	46.5	76.9	42.0	50.0	100.0	-
2.	25.0	25.0	13.1	23.1	17.4	5.0	-	25.0
3.	10.9	50.0	20.2	-	4.4	10.0	-	-
4.	10.9	25.0	3.0	-	20.3	10.0	-	-
5.	14.1	-	17.2	-	15.9	25.0	-	75.0
Total	100.0 (N = 64)[a]	100.0 (N = 12)	100.0 (N = 99)	100.0 (N = 13)	100.0 (N = 69)	100.0 (N = 20)	100.0 (N = 10)	100.0 (N = 4)

Distance Zone	Transient Situational O.P. %	Transient Situational Crisis Clinic %	Undiagnosed O.P. %	Undiagnosed Crisis Clinic %	Other Inc. Organic O.P. %	Other Inc. Organic Crisis Clinic %	All Diagnoses O.P. %	All Diagnoses Crisis Clinic %
1.	27.0	-	41.5	-	-	-	42.8	34.0
2.	18.7	-	24.9	-	100.0	-	18.3	13.5
3.	12.5	50.0	16.6	50.0	-	-	12.4	22.0
4.	21.8	50.0	16.6	50.0	-	-	11.4	17.0
5.	18.7	-	-	-	-	-	14.9	13.5
Total	100.0 (N = 32)	100.0 (N = 6)	100.0 (N = 12)	100.0 (N = 4)	100.0 (N = 3)	-	100.0 (N = 289)	100.0 (N = 59)

[a] Frequencies standardized for variations in population sizes of distance zones.

standardized relative frequencies of patients completing four or more therapeutic sessions will decrease with increasing distance; and that the more complex
the diagnosis, the more important it will be to the patient to obtain therapy,
thus the influence of distance on proportionate use will be less important.

Analysis of the data reveals that there is a proportionate decline in use of
these mental health services with distance, supporting the first hypothesis. As
was the case with preceeding analysis, use of outpatient clinics is more heavily
inversely influenced by the distance to the service than is use of the Crisis Clinic.
However, the influence of distance on proportionate numbers of admissions who
complete four or more sessions varies relativley little among the several diagnoses
for which there are relatively large numbers of observations.

The spatial distribution of people using conventional outpatient clinical
services is comparable for patients diagnosed as psychotic, psychoneurotic, or
having personality disorders. In some contrast, proportional figures for the group
diagnosed as transient situational or adjustment reactions demonstrate that
clients travel further to outpatient clinics to receive assistance with this problem
condition. As discussed earlier, most of these latter patients are referred by a
social agency, and the recommendation of a particular source of care appears to
influence the greater distance these clients travel. Because the first two of the
four conditions mentioned tend to be the most complex and often the most
debilitating, the pattern of use of outpatient clinics by clients with various
presented problems tends to refute the second hypothesis identified above.

The Crisis Clinic appears to draw clients diagnosed as psychotic or with
transient situational disturbances further than it does patients with other
presented problems. The major exception to this pattern is the group of clients
evaluated as psychoneurotic, who come entirely from the first two distance
zones. It should be noted that the number of observations for these groups are
relatively small, suggesting the need for caution in drawing inferences from these
data.

A major conclusion to be drawn from this analysis is that diagnosis does not
appear to be a very important intervening variable with reference to the
influence of distance on willingness to consume therapeutic services provided by
either outpatient clinics or the Crisis Clinic. Further, distance generally has a
similar enough influence on use of either type of service that the lambdas for the
prediction of one given the other, by diagnosis, were usually zero or very small.

Use of the Nearest Clinical Mental Health Agency

In addition to analyzing the general effect of distance on choice of clinics, a
complementary approach concerns the extent to which consumers pass one
center on their way to another center, or travel to a more distant center rather

than using the one closest to their place of residence. Furthermore, we may assess whether the influence of such intervening opportunities differs for patients from various racial groups. For this analysis, the census tracts of the Westside District were grouped on the basis of the outpatient clinic physically closest to them.

Patients residing in census tracts located closest to a given clinic are found to use that clinic relatively more frequently than any other, more distant source of outpatient service. However, black clients located closest to California Psychiatric Clinic and to St. Mary's constitute the only cases in which outpatient centers received the majority (75 and 60 percent respectively) of the closest patients. The median proportional attractiveness of closest clinics is 33 percent, or only about one-third of the consumers of outpatient services utilize the nearest center.

While small frequencies of clients from some neighboring areas encourage exercising caution in interpreting the results of this analysis, racial differences do appear to be substantial. White patients have a relatively constant rate of utilizing the closest clinic. Rates of use of second nearest centers often equal or approach the proportion of white patients attracted to the closest clinical service. Black clients, on the other hand, use some agencies which are physically most accessible to them at rates exceeding those for white clients by from sixteen to forty-eight points, and other closest centers not at all. Black patients are found to favor the outpatient clinics at Mt. Zion and St. Mary's Hospitals, regardless of other clinics which are closer.[f]

Summary and Conclusions

Analysis discussed in this chapter has dealt with the influence of physical accessibility on general revealed demand for clinical mental health services, on the differential use of Westside Center Services provided by conventional outpatient clinics and by the Crisis Clinic, and on the consumer behavior of clients from various groups. No clear pattern of the influence of distance on use of the several outpatient clinics emerged, but the lambda for clinics at given distances suggests that accessibility accounts for approximately 14 percent of the choice of clinic. An unexpected result was a slight increase in demand, standardized for variations in population, for services at the Crisis Clinic as distances increased.

When data for the several outpatient clinics were combined, it was found that use of these clinics was more sensitive to increases in distance than was use of

---

[f]Since most of the black population of the Westside District lives in Census Area J, these two agencies appear to have locations most central to the activity space of these residents. See "Social Structuring of Space" in Chapter 2 for a discussion of the role played by activity space in influencing the consumption of health services.

the Crisis Clinic and that physical distance accounts for 30 percent of the variation in the use of these two categories of service. Aggregation of data concerning the use of services provided by outpatient centers also resulted in an exponential decay curve for porportionate use with increasing distance, in contrast to a bimodal distribution for the Crisis Clinic. Similarly, withdrawals were found to proportionately exceed discharges at outpatient clinics in the furthest distance zones, but not for the Crisis Clinic.

Disaggregation of the client population by racial group membership revealed substantial differences in the influence of distance on utilization of services. While the relative frequency of use by white patients declined with distance for both outpatient clinics and the Crisis Clinic, black and Mexican-American use of conventional outpatient services were more heavily negatively influenced by decreasing accessibility. On the other hand, proportionate use of the Crisis Clinic by individuals from these latter two groups substantially increased with distance, apparently as a result of the attractiveness of services provided only at this center.

While more patients tend to choose the most accessible outpatient clinic over any other outpatient clinic, use of the closest clinic accounts for only about one-third of all outpatient clinic clients. This indicates the relative importance of other variables influencing demand, in addition to consumer tendencies to minimize trip-making costs.

In summary, analysis of data on consumer behavior demonstrates that distance has the effect of a cost imposed on users of outpatient clinics, and that this influence of distance varies among consumer groups. However, distance is found to account for a minor proportion of the variation in consumer choice of the clinic to patronize. The following chapter treats other factors which help to explain consumer behavior in using outpatient mental health services.

8

The Influence of Type and
Delivery of Clinical Services on
the Behavior of Westside
Mental Health Center Clients

Another major category of supply characteristic which is expected to affect demand for mental health care is the form of the therapeutic service provided. Types of therapeutic intervention, as discussed in Chapter 3, may be distinguished as to whether interview sessions are group or individual, the theory informing the therapist's treatment pattern, and other similar dimensions. We are especially interested here, however, in a programmatic composite of characteristics which typify major forms of outpatient service provided by the Westside Mental Health Center.

The first major classification of services supplied to ambulatory patients separates the Crisis Clinic from other outpatient clinics in Westside. While a number of patients at the Crisis Clinic do arrive while their psychiatric disability is especially acute, many more appear to use this agency for short-term therapy for a nonemergency condition. The Crisis Clinic provides immediate counseling, the therapy is primarily supportive, and the therapist responds to symptoms rather than becoming involved in lengthy diagnosis. Clients may use the Crisis Clinic for up to six visits for an episode of mental illness, after which they are referred to an outpatient clinic. In other words, the type of service and the administration of the Crisis Clinic encourages short-term use and does not require extensive commitment by the client to the demands of thoroughgoing psychotherapy. The Crisis Clinic opened in early 1969, midway through the period for which client data was assembled for this study.

In contrast, outpatient psychiatric clinics provide longer-term therapy, with no arbitrary limit on the number of visits permitted. The service is more oriented toward securing a lasting cure and is more heavily dependent on the diagnosis to inform prescription of a therapeutic program for a patient. Clients are sometimes referred from the Crisis Clinic, but usually seek their first admission directly to the outpatient clinic of their choice.

Outpatient clinics may be differentiated further by characteristics of the service which they provide. Some of the outpatient clinics in Westside have waiting lists requiring patients to delay their entry into therapy for a week or more. The outpatient clinic at Pacific Presbyterian Hospital required three days of psychological testing for diagnostic purposes. Several of the clinics are units of hospitals which are associated with religious groups. Finally, some of the clinics appear to specialize in providing services for specific groups of clients such as children or private patients.

The major questions we seek to answer in this chapter are how and to what extent do differences in the type of service provided affect the utilization of these services? Additionally, how do various client groups respond differently to these services? Among clinics offering largely the same service, what effects do recognizable differences between the clinics appear to have on their utilization? Finally, what was the impact of the addition of the Crisis Clinic as an alternative source of mental health service for Westside residents on the utilization of outpatient clinics serving the area?

Influence of Major Types of Psychiatric Services on Utilization

The effect on demand for psychiatric care of major types of service, represented here by the Crisis Clinic on the one hand and the outpatient clinics on the other, may be directly assessed by examining the proportions of clients using these agencies. Of all clients first admitted during the three sample months from 1969/70, 39 percent used the Crisis Clinic and 61 percent sought assistance at the five outpatient clinics.

If each of the six agencies supplying mental health services to ambulatory patients were equally attractive, each would be expected to receive an equal share of the patients—about 16.7 percent of the first admissions from this period. The Crisis Clinic accounted for more than twice the expected demand based on the above assumption. Furthermore, the Crisis Clinic received 49 percent of all first admissions (N = 413) recorded for March 1970, the sample month for the second year that this service was provided. This proportion is almost three times the figure expected if the services provided by each of the six agencies were equally attractive.

While this demonstrates the popularity of the service package supplied by the Crisis Clinic, it should be realized that the proportionate distribution of revealed demand would probably differ if this type of service were available from more than a single agency. In other words, these data suggest that the two major types of mental health service currently available are approximately equally attractive. If the type of service supplied at the Crisis Clinic was available at multiple locations and was consequently more accessible, it appears likely that it would attract more than half of the people seeking ambulatory psychiatric assistance.

One measure of the relative effectiveness of the two types of service is the lasting effect of the treatment. An index of this effectiveness is the proportionate rate of readmission for patients receiving each type of therapy. For the three months representing 1969/70, 90.5 percent of the people treated by outpatient clinics were not readmitted, while the comparable figure for the Crisis Clinic was 75 percent, a 15 percent difference. Furthermore, patients first treated by the Crisis Clinic account for the substantial majority of those individuals who were readmitted to therapeutic services either once or twice before July 1970, when the data for this study was collected.

While this finding is expected, given the short-term therapeutic service offered at the Crisis Clinic, it should be remembered that clients may only receive six treatment sessions at this center, and that the Crisis Clinic is intended as an intake and referral service for other agencies which are members of Westside Mental Health Center. However, as was noted earlier, only 9.3 percent of the patients using the Crisis Clinic were referred to other psychiatric services, including hospitalization. Secondly, some therapeutic assistance and continued availability of the service when it is desired is probably more congruent with the lifestyles and values of some individuals.[1] Longer-term therapy, which when completed ends the client's demand for mental health care, requires behavior which would be unacceptable to these patients.

In other words, therapy which encourages consecutive admissions as desired appears to be the most effective form of mental health service for some groups of clients. This appears to be the nature of the service supplied by the Crisis Clinic. On the other hand, more traditional psychotherapy provided at outpatient clinics appears to have a more lasting effect, as indicated by the high proportion of clients using this form of service who do not seek readmission.

Differences in Client Group Responses to Major Types of Psychiatric Services

Similar analysis of the magnitude and relative frequency of demand for services provided by the Crisis Clinic and by all other agencies is useful for assessing differences in the responses of various client groups. Earlier discussion concerning the effect of accessibility on utilization of mental health services revealed that clients tended to travel greater distances for the type of service available at the Crisis Clinic than to the more conventional outpatient mental health clinics (Tables 7-4 and 7-5). It was also demonstrated that black and Mexican-American clients assumed considerably greater trip-making costs to secure services at the Crisis Clinic than would have been required by using closer outpatient clinics.

Approximately two-thirds of the black (N = 265) and Mexican-American (N = 26) clients first admitted to Westside Center agencies during the three sample months for 1969/70 chose to use the Crisis Clinic. Only one-third of the white clients (N = 737) chose this agency, while about one-tenth more of the Oriental clients (N = 14) use the Crisis Clinic. Proportionately, black and Mexican-American clients choose to seek service at the Crisis Clinic twice as frequently as did white clients. Clearly, the service package offered by the Crisis Clinic is preferred by current black and Mexican-American consumers of ambulatory mental health services over the service package available at the five outpatient clinics.

As a consequence of these patterns of utilization by clients from the several racial groups, white clients account for three-quarters of the patients seen at outpatient clinics, but only 55 percent of those admitted by the Crisis Clinic. Black and Mexican-American clients are proportionately more than twice as frequent as patients at the Crisis Clinic than at the outpatient clinics. Clients from these two racial minority groups accounted for more than 40 percent of the first admissions to the Crisis Clinic during the three sample months representing 1969/70.

Earlier analysis of consumer behavior based on demographic characteristics of clients showed that people using the Crisis Clinic are preportionately more frequently between the ages of twenty-one and forty, and over the age of seventy, than is the case for all outpatients admitted during the three sample months for 1969/70. It was also noted that males constitute the majority of clients only at the Crisis Clinic. Explanation of these findings emphasized the unique characteristics of the service provided by the Crisis Clinic and the availability of service during hours which facilitate its use by people who are employed.

Influence of Differences among Outpatient Clinics on Utilization of Services by Various Client Groups

The type of psychiatric service provided by the outpatient clinics has been differentiated from the therapy available at the Crisis Clinic. The preceeding analysis revealed that the characteristics of these two types of service, and the differences in demands which they place on clients, result in differences in the characteristics of the client population of each, how far the clients are willing to travel to each, and the relative frequency with which each is used.

Some analogous differences exist among the several outpatient clinics. Although each of these clinics provide longer-term analytical therapy, each has one or more major service features or characteristics which appear to result in the service received at each being viewed by the client as inequivalent to that available at the others. Differences in the relative use of the various outpatient clinics would support this hypothesis. To the extent that popularly recognized differences are correctly identified for purposes of analysis, the relative frequency with which a clinic is used would also indicate the importance of that clinic's corresponding characteristics in influencing consumer behavior.

The most prominent characteristic of this sort is the religious affiliation or identity of the hospital at which the clinic is located. Previous findings concerning the tendency of patients to select "compatable" hospitals were discussed in Chapter 2. Of the five outpatient clinics, St. Mary's is Catholic, Pacific Medical Center is Presbyterian, and Mt. Zion is Jewish. Data on the religion of people using Westside Center services are not available, precluding matching clients and hospitals by this characteristic. However, it appears reasonable to conclude that few of the black clients are Jewish or Catholic, and that Mexican-American clients are predominately Catholic. As cited earlier, some information is available concerning residential concentrations of several ethnic groups.

The various outpatient agencies also differ with respect to intake and admission characteristics. St. Mary's and Children's Hospitals have similar intake procedures in that walk-in patients will usually be seen and receive an appointment to begin therapy within twenty-four hours. Mt. Zion Outpatient Clinic, on the other hand, normally has a waiting list of from one to three weeks. At Pacific Medical Center, the intake procedure was exceptionally long, involving three days of psychological testing. This practice was in operation through March 1970, but has since been discontinued.

The information which individuals have about available services probably also influences consumer behavior. For example, the clinic at Children's Hospital provides outpatient services for adults as well as younger clients, but it appears that the availability of this service is not widely known. Similarly, some prospective clients probably do not know that St. Mary's clinic is open and will receive individuals seeking help any time, twenty-four hours a day, somewhat as does the Crisis Clinic.

Finally, all but one of the outpatient clinics provided therapeutic services at subsidized or no cost to clients with family incomes of $750 or less a month, during the 1968 through 1970 period represented by data used in this study. Short-Doyle funds, which have since been cut off, covered the full cost of service to very low-income individuals and underwrote the prices charged other clients based on their income. California Medical Clinic for Psychotherapy was the only Westside Center member agency for which Short-Doyle funding was not available. Here, patients paid fees ranging from about $30 to about $15 per therapeutic session, based on their income. Patients at other clinics with self-reported family incomes of over $750 were required to pay the full cost, which commonly meant prices higher than those charged by private psychiatrists.

Characteristics of outpatient clinics such as the ones just cited are expected to have differing effects on various groups of clients in influencing their consumption behavior. Analysis of this behavior requires the presentation of some data in addition to that discussed earlier in this study. Preceeding tables will be used when these are appropriate.

The relative distribution of clients by racial group membership among the outpatient clinics provides information concerning which of the agencies are especially favored as sources of service by each group. Each clinic would be expected to receive about 20 percent of the total number of clients from each group if the clinics were equally attractive. Table 8-1 demonstrates that this is not the case. The clinic at St. Mary's Hospital is disproportionately favored by all racial groups, followed in popularity by Mt. Zion, while Children's Hospital sees the smallest percentage of all groups except one.

Table 8-1
Distribution of Clients, by Race, among Outpatient Clinics, First Admissions for
Three Sample Months, 1969/70[a]

| | Agency | | | | | |
Race of Client	Cal. Med. %	Children's %	Mt. Zion %	PMC %	St. Mary's %	Total %
Caucasian	23.6	8.6	20.6	8.8	38.4	100.0 (N = 499)
Black	8.6	6.7	25.7	10.5	48.6	100.0 (N = 105)
Mexican-American	0.0	12.5	12.5	25.0	50.0	100.0 (N = 8)
Oriental	37.5	0.0	12.5	0.0	0.0	100.0 (N = 8)

[a]Does not include 54 patients for whom information on race is not available, and 430
patients admitted at the Crisis Clinic during these three sample months.

Whites utilize St. Mary's about twice as frequently as expected, while PMC
and Children's receive less than half of their proportional share. First admissions
of whites to Cal. Med. and Mt. Zion during these three sample months were at
expected levels. Black clients proportionately favored St. Mary's and Mt. Zion,
while the other three clinics received one-half to one-third the expected number
of first admissions from this group. Mexican-Americans showed preferences for
St. Mary's and PMC, while Orientals predominately used St. Mary's and Cal.
Med. The total number of observations for each of these last two groups of
clients is so small that further analysis of these data is of doubtful value.

The disproportionately large use of the clinic at St. Mary's Hospital by all
racial groups may be explained in part by its relatively central location within
the catchment, and by the short waiting time involved in securing service. St.
Mary's Hospital is one of several Catholic institutions forming the nucleus for a
residential concentration of Catholic families. This is a probable explanation for
the earlier finding that the clinic at St. Mary's has the highest proportion (36
percent) of white clients from that part of the catchment closest to it of any
Westside Center member agency. However, the exceptionally high proportion of
Mexican-American clients selecting this clinic (Table 8-1) is the only clear case of
religious compatibility which analysis of this data will support.

Earlier analysis of the sex distribution of use revealed the overall proportional
dominance of females among the clients of clinical services, with the exception
of the Crisis Clinic. Disproportionate use of the Crisis Clinic by men was
explained as a function of their greater demand for short-term therapy and the
convenience of open hours offered by this facility. St. Mary's offers longer-term
therapy but also provides service on a twenty-four hour, walk-in basis. Yet males
account for only about 45 percent of the clients at this agency, a proportion
similar to that for other outpatient agencies.

This characteristic of St. Mary's service probably accounts for part of its popularity; it received 22.8 percent of the first admissions to all six Westside Center agencies during the three sample months for 1969/70. However, availability of service after regular working hours does not have the expected result of its being used more frequently by men than by women.

Information concerning the availability of service on a twenty-four hour basis is probably most accessible to those residents of the catchment living in the vicinity of the clinic at St. Mary's. This hypothesis is supported by the findings that, of the Westside Center member clinics, St. Mary's has the largest proportion of all patients (60.3 percent) coming from its closest distance zone (Table 7-1), and unusually low proportions coming from its furthest three distance zones. Additionally, 86 percent of the black clients using St. Mary's come from its two closest concentric distance zones, which is the highest proportion from these two zones for any clinic.

Despite a longer waiting period between being admitted and receiving treatment, Mt. Zion is the second most frequently used of the outpatient clinics for the three sample months (Table 8-2). While the length of the waiting list is seen as a cost which would cause an agency to appear relatively less atractive to clients, it may also be interpreted as an index of the relatively greater attractiveness of the services provided by that agency. The latter appear to be the case for both black and white clients using Mt. Zion.

Inpatient and outpatient psychiatric services provided at Mt. Zion have outstanding reputations for being of high quality. Furthermore, black residents of the Filmore District have identified Mt. Zion as the agency with which to push demands for services which they perceive as appropriate to their needs. As a result, Mt. Zion sees a smaller proportion of white patients than do the other outpatient clinics (Table 8-2). It should be noted that the racial group membership for almost 27 percent of the first admissions for three months at Mt. Zion were unrecorded. It is probable that most of these clients were black,

Table 8-2

Patient Populations of Outpatient Clinics, by Race, First Admissions for Three Sample Months, 1969/70

| | Agency | | | | |
Race of Client	Cal. Med. %	Children's %	Mt. Zion %	PMC %	St. Mary's %
Caucasian	90.1	81.1	57.2	77.2	76.1
Black	6.9	13.2	15.0	19.3	20.3
Mexican-American	0.0	1.9	0.6	3.5	1.6
Oriental	2.3	0.0	0.6	0.0	1.6
Other or Unknown	0.7	3.8	26.6	0.0	0.4
Total	100.0	100.0	100.0	100.0	100.0
	(N = 131)	(N = 53)	(N = 180)	(N = 57)	(N = 251)

which would give Mt. Zion a higher proportion of clients from this racial group than the comparable figure for any other outpatient clinic.

The highest proportion of white clients using Mt. Zion come from the nearest distance zone. This immediate area accounts for 20 percent more of the first admissions to this clinic than does the nearest zone for PMC, the agency with the next largest comparable figure. The next two distance zones account for unusually low proportions of these clients. Mt. Zion draws the second highest proportion of its patients (29.4 percent) from the area closer to it than to any other clinic. In other words, Mt. Zion especially serves white clients living close to the clinic, an area which appears to have a disproportionatley large Jewish population.

Black clients of Mt. Zion live predominately in the second through fourth distance zones. While they travel proportionately further to this clinic than do whites, about half of the black clients live in zone two, which includes Filmore. This appears to reflect the decision by this group to make this agency a major source of therapeutic services.

The racial composition of the clientele at Mt. Zion suggests a further hypothesis; that various demographic groups, separated by considerable social distance, resist joint use of facilities supplying mental health services. If this is the case, then utilization of mental health services might be increased by providing services at separate centers for each major public residing in the catchment; that is, providing the services in a pluralistic manner. The Mt. Zion clients for whom race is unrecorded make this hypothesis difficult to test. A major argument against the tactic of providing separate clinics is that the poor will not be able to successfully attract the financial and especially the manpower resources required to provide the services needed.[2]

The unexpectedly low proportions of both black and white clients using PMC (Table 8-1) tends to suuport the hypothesis that the lengthy intake procedure influences consumer behavior. The residential distribution of white patients using PMC approximates a distance decay curve, demonstrating that closeness to the clinic plays an important role in its choice by this group.

The small number of black patients seeking therapy from this agency predominately come from the most remote of the distance zones, which include areas occupied by the wealthier residents of the catchment. These patients do not appear to be discouraged from using PMC by the three days of testing that were a required part of admissions.

The relative age distribution of clients at PMC, when compared with those for other agencies, tends to further illustrate the role of the intake procedure in influencing consumer selection. During the three sample months, PMC had few first admissions from the sixteen-to-twenty-year-old age group, while 93.9 percent of its clients were from the groups spanning the ages twenty-one through fifty. This was about six points above the similar figure for Cal. Med., the agency with the next highest proportion of its patients from these age groups. To the extent that younger clients are less patient with a lengthy admission process, this finding further supports the hypothesis that extensive psychological testing influenced some groups of Westside Center clients to consider other clinics as more attractive sources of therapeutic services.

California Medical Clinic for Psychotherapy is predominately differentiated from the other outpatient clinics by its prices. It was established as a private clinic to provide primarily long-term therapy, and while it receives some federal money for staffing, it has not sought state Short-Doyle funds for underwriting patient fees. Over 90 percent of the clients at Cal. Med. are white, a proportion which exceeds that for any other Westside Center agency by nine points. It sees substantially less than half the proportion of black clients treated by most of the other outpatient clinics. The unusual racial composition of the client population at Cal. Med. appears to be a result of its pricing policy.

While almost 70 percent of the admissions to Cal. Med. for the three sample months were individuals living in its two closest distance zones (Table 7-1), the second and fifth zones accounted for relatively large portions of its white patients. Similarly, proportions of its black patients coming from its first, second, and fifth distance zones are unusually large when compared with the spatial distributions of patients using other clinics. Of the clinics, California attracts the highest proportion (75 percent) of all black patients from the area closer to it than to any other clinic.

In the cases of both black and white patients, these are relatively high income areas. Since clients using Cal. Med. could not obtain treatment at Short-Doyle subsidized prices based on their income, it is not surprising that selection of this clinic by clients from each of these groups appears to be related to income. Furthermore, the perceived quality of the therapeutic service available at this clinic appears to result in comparatively high proportions of patients traveling further to this clinic than do clients of other agencies.

The outpatient psychiatric services available at Children's Hospital since 1968 resemble those provided by the several other clinics. However, Children's had no waiting list during the three sample months for 1969/70, had a simple intake procedure, and clients could receive Short-Doyle subsidies. While its services are most comparable to those offered at St. Mary's, in marked contrast Children's accounts for only 4.8 percent of the observations for 1969/70. Its fifty-three new patients for these months gave it the smallest group of clients admitted by any clinic for this period.

A major reason for this phenomenon appears to be that the availability of adult outpatient services at this agency is largely unknown among the population of the catchment. This conclusion is partially supported by the importance of referrals from medical services which, as pointed out earlier, constituted half as many sources of admission to this agency as self-referrals (Table 6-2).

This explanation of the proportionate underutilization of outpatient services at Children's is further supported by the finding that females accounted for 66.1

percent of Children's clients for the 1969/70 sample months, approximately 13 percent more than the proportion of women using all Westside clinical services. This suggests that women taking children to this hospital obtained special information about the availability of services for adults, or were encouraged to receive counseling in connection with psychiatric care being provided to their children. The disproportionate use of this agency by women, and the relation of use by this group to services sought by women for their children, supports the hypothesis that adult psychotherapeutic services available at Children's Hospital are not widely known about by residents of Westside.

Both the importance of referrals and the connection between a high proportion of female use and therapy sought for children are supported by analysis of clients' residential distribution. Large proportions of white patients come from distance zones three, four, and five;[a] and two, three, and five are the only zones of origin for black patients. This suggests that clients travel further than would be necessary if they willingly used the clinic located closest to them and that referral resulting in a multipurpose trip influences the choice of clinic by those who use Children's Hospital.[b]

In summary, consumers' choices among the five outpatient clinics do appear to be influenced by the characteristics of the services provided at these clinics. These service characteristics also tend to influence the behavior of various client groups differently. In other words, characteristics which differentiate the services provided at the various clinics are seen as important determinants of "service areas" for these clinics, or who comes from where to use these clinics. Previously identified determinants of this sort from medical services research include accessibility, reputation of the agency, referrals, and ethnic or personal ties.[3] The preceeding analysis adds to this list factors including relative user charges, information concerning availability of services, intake procedures, and the delay between admission and securing therapy because of waiting lists.

Support of hypotheses concerning the manner in which features of the programs at the various clinics affect choices has been derived from analysis of data concerning current user behavior. However, the relative importance of these characteristics in influencing choices is more difficult to infer from these data. Information concerning the latter would be obtained most appropriately and more directly by asking clients about the bases of their choices; then tradeoffs between alternative program characteristics could be made, possibly using a semiprojective game. Interviews of this nature require resource which were not available for this research project.

---

[a]Of the clients using the clinic at Children's Hospital, 81 percent are Caucasian, the second highest proportion for the five outpatient clinics.

[b]The lambda coefficient of correlation for choice of agency given source of referral is 0.397, suggesting that the means of referral heavily influences the choice of the center used. Information available to agents making referrals probably plays an important role in the choice of the clinic at Children's Hospital.

Effects of the Crisis Clinic on Utilization of Outpatient Clinics

As noted in the introduction to this section, the Crisis Clinic began operations in early 1969. In light of the importance of this clinic in providing psychiatric services to Westside Center clients, and given its exceptional attractiveness as a source of service for clients with particular demographic characteristics, it is important to assess the impact of this new service on the continuing use of outpatient clinics. The working hypothesis is that the Crisis Clinic has not taken over or decreased demand for services provided by outpatient clinics. This hypothesis may be tested by comparing the numbers and proportions of first admissions to outpatient clinics for the sample months from 1968, before the Crisis Clinic was established , with comparable data for 1969/70, the period during which the Crisis Clinic was operating. This comparison is only possible for four out of the five outpatient clinics, because 1968 data for the clinic at St. Mary's Hospital are not available.

The percentage changes in total admissions at the various outpatient clinics since the organization of Westside Mental Health Center and the Crisis Clinic are substantial. Monthly average first admissions increased by 26.7 percent for Cal. Med. between 1968 and 1969/70, 60.9 percent for Children's, 37.9 percent for Mt. Zion, and 52 percent for PMC. Demand for services at each of the outpatient clinics has increased since the opening of the Crisis Clinic, by from a quarter to over one-half of the previous rates for first admissions. Similarly, the proportion of clients who are black has increased for most outpatient clinics since the establishment of the Crisis Clinic.

Also, the lengths of trips made by clients to obtain psychiatric services have decreased since the introduction of the Crisis Clinic. The proportion of white patients traveling from distance zones four and five to Cal. Med. and Children's Hospital declined by over twenty-three points, as did patients from zone five using Mt. Zion. Similarly, the proportion of black patients from zones three and four using Children's Hospital and from zone four using Mt. Zion declined by over twenty-five points. Mexican-Americans using Mt. Zion continued to come from zone four and at the same rate. With the exception of Mt. Zion, which had a decrease in the standardized frequency of black patients for 1969/70 and continued to have the same frequency of Mexican-American patients, all centers increased in the absolute numbers of patients by racial group admitted per month.

These changes have resulted in a wider distribution of patients from each racial group among agencies. As a consequence, these clients have recently tended to use more accessible outpatient centers with increasing frequency. Longer trips, especially for black and Mexican-American patients, appear to have shifted from outpatient centers to the Crisis Clinic. For reasons such as improved information and substitution of short-term for long-term therapy, distances traveled to outpatient centers have tended to decrease for patients from all racial groups.

While the frequency of admissions to the Crisis Clinic has grown rapidly, to the extent that this agency accounted for nearly 43 percent of the total first admissions in March 1970, the numbers of people seeking therapy at outpatient clinics have also increased. Assuming that the incidence of mental illness for the Westside population remained constant during this three-year period, the increase in revealed demand for services of outpatient clinics appears to have been primarily influenced by greater public awareness and acceptance of available services through publicity concerning the establishment of Westside Mental Health Center and as a result of opening the Crisis Clinic.

Summary and Conclusions

Two major kinds of therapy are provided on an outpatient basis by Westside Center. These are the short-term, low-commitment services offered by the Crisis Clinic, and longer-term, more conventional therapy available at outpatient clinics. Popularity of the first of these has resulted in the Crisis Clinic accounting for about 40 percent of the first admissions, with the balance distributed among the five agencies providing the second type of service package.

Popularity of the Crisis Clinic as the source of therapy varies by racial group membership. While about two-thirds of the black and Mexican-American clients first admitted during three sample months chose to use the Crisis Clinic, less than one-thrid of the white patients and just over two-fifths of the Oriental clients selected this agency.

The outpatient clinics differ on the basis of characteristics of the services which they provide. The clinic at St. Mary's Hospital received an unexpectedly large number of first admissions during the three sample months, probably as a result of its central location, Catholic affiliation, rapid intake procedures, and possibly its twenty-four hour availability. Mt. Zion, the second most frequently used outpatient center, is widely known as a source of high quality care and has been identified among black residents of the adjacent areas as a cooperative agency.

The lengthy intake procedures at Pacific Medical Center during the sample months appears to discourage use by younger consumers, and the pricing policy at Cal. Med. seems to result in its predominately serving clients from the higher income residential areas located in the Westside District. Unexpectedly light utilization of the clinic at Children's Hospital probably results from lack of general knowledge that adult psychotherapy is available from this agency. Several of the service characteristics which were identified in this analysis as having an influence on consumer behavior do not appear to have been treated by previous research on health or mental health care.

Finally, comparison of data on first admissions for 1968 and for 1969/70 demonstrate that establishment of the Crisis Clinic at the beginning of 1969 has not decreased demand for services at outpatient clinics. However, several shifts in the racial composition of the clientele at various clinics are observed. These shifts have generally resulted in a more even distribution of black and white clients among the outpatient clinics.

9

Suggestions for Further Research

The analysis reported in the four preceeding chapters has identified a number of features which differentiate the outpatient service packages supplied by various agencies belonging to Westside Mental Health Center. This analysis has also shown how various user groups differ in their responses to these service packages.

These findings begin to demonstrate that revealed demand for a public service of this sort is, at least in part, a function of several characteristics of that service. For purposes of policy analysis, this suggests the possibility of identifying characteristics which prospective consumers find attractive and incorporating these into the design of the service in order to encourage its increased utilization. This use of consumer analysis is a form of client-oriented planning, as discussed in the opening section of Chapter 2.

This approach to planning pulic services is becoming widely accepted in principle. However, the technical means to perform such planning in a replicable manner have not been available.[1] Major purposes of this study have been to explore and elaborate on the consumer-analysis approach to planning and to contribute to the development of ways in which it can be done. Considerably more research remains before an operational and reliable set of methods for this form of planning are in hand.

The recent of work of several economists has pointed up a promising direction for this additional required research. Out of this work has emerged what may be called an *abstract approach* for analyzing goods and consumer responses to them. In the discussion which follows, this abstract approach is reviewed and its promise as a framework for further research is assessed. By way of illustrating the application of this approach, some analytical definitions of outpatient mental health services, based on the empirical work in this study, are also developed.

An Abstract Approach to Goods and Consumer Responses

Development of a new approach to consumer theory observes the deficiencies of traditional theory in dealing unanalytically with goods.[2] Most economic theory views goods as the direct objects of utility. By focusing instead on the properties or characteristics[3] of the good which provides the consumer with utility, various

121

substitution or complementary goods may be evaluated as to the bases of their relative attractiveness.

Furthermore, consumer evaluation of new commodities may be derived from data on responses to characteristics held in common with various previously available commodities. Thus goods that are effectively substitutes need not be considered as separate goods or as the same good with differences disregarded, but "goods associated with satisfaction vectors which differ in only one component,"[4] or at most a limited number of such components. Using this new perspective, Lancaster develops the notion of a "consumption technology,"[5] involving combining goods on the basis of the contribution of their characteristics, to support a given level of desired activity.

In the case of consumer behavior with respect to alternative outpatient mental health service packages, this approach lends itself to analyzing the contributions to satisfaction made by each service package on the basis of its performance on each of several characteristics dimensions. Some alternative outpatient services are not close substitutes such as a service requiring a complex intake procedure absent at other centers. In this case, it appears that the consumers weigh the various combinations of characteristics, which functionally define the different services, in reaching their decision.

Where various consumer groups respond differently to a service package, these responses may be evaluated as differential weighting of performance with respect to the associated characteristics' dimensions. Also, when a group evaluates and chooses a service on the basis of several characteristics but not others, this approach explains why changes in the performance or price of these other characteristics will not affect demand.

As Lancaster points out, this model is "very many times richer in heuristic explanatory and predictive power than the conventional model of consumer behavior and [is] one that deals easily with those many commonsense characteristics of actual behavior that have found no place in traditional exposition."[6]

In a direct application, Quandt and Baumol assess alternative means of interurban transportation as abstract modes, each typified by a set of performance characteristics, rather than using conventional examples.[7] This approach serves two purposes. Measures of relative performance with respect to various characteristics can be used instead of dealing with direct measures of features such as comfort. Secondly, this approach permits prediction of the effect of introducing a new mode of transportation on demand for every existing mode. To accomplish this, the new mode is specified by its performance characteristics, and total demand is forecast as a function of a set of old and new transportation modes.

This model assumes no bias on the part of consumers favoring or disfavoring the various modes. Choice then depends on the absolute performance level of the "best" mode with respect to each criterion or characteristic dimension and the relative performance of other modes on these same criteria.[8]

A similar application of this approach aids in analyzing consumer response to alternative mental health service packages. The service packages, or outpatient service offered by each agency or clinic, are the counterparts of Quandt and Baumol's modes. The features of the service package design, such as accessibility of the center and attitude or quality of the staff, are criteria or performance characteristics.[a] As each of the service packages are assessed by the prospective consumer, the characteristics of these alternatives are evaluated in relative terms.

Some Characteristics of Outpatient Mental Health Service Packages

Abstract analysis of service packages requires identification of the characteristics of these packages to which consumers respond. The following discussion seeks to identify several of these characteristics, notes some additional research dealing with these, and suggests some promising modifications of the way in which outpatient services might be designed in order to increase their utilization.

Not only is psychiatric intervention or treatment a complex intermediate service, but consumers must make a number of subchoices in gaining access to the service. We will consider both the process of obtaining the service and the service itself as a single service package, having a number of characteristics or criterion to which persons respond in making a decision concerning whether, where, when, and how much to consume. For purposes of exposition, these characteristics are grouped into clusters relating to mode of therapy, services provided by an agency, characteristics of the facility, relative location of the supply point, and price.

Mode of Therapy

The first of these groups of characteristics is the mode of therapy, which in the case of outpatients may consist of several combinations of treatments. These treatments were discussed in Chapter 3, and the point was made that the therapist largely determines the combination to be used, based on a diagnosis of the client's distress, resources, and attitudes toward therapy.[10] Thus the client may influence the prescription by registering preferences, and may refuse to follow the prescribed therapeutic procedure. The outpatient client may also choose between psychiatric therapy intended to change the existing condition

---

[a]Baumol has applied this general approach to developing an optimizing strategy for a firm in seeking a larger market through differential allocation to various store or good attributes, proposing the use of linear integer programming. The retail establishment is analyzed as a bundle of attributes, and consumers are grouped into classes responding to one subset of these attributes rather than another. A similar strategy may be employed by agencies providing outpatient mental health services to increase consumer demand by various subpopulations of a catchment area.[9]

and develop means for dealing with stress in the future, or elect to use the Crisis Clinic, whic provides services to help deal with the immediate problem and places little emphasis on long-range effect. Thus ameliorative therapy aimed at changing the psychiatric condition of an individual usually requires a longer-term program of treatment and greater commitment than does adaptive or supportive assistance.

Services Provided by an Agency

Characteristics of the agency service includes the intake procedure, the apparent expertise of the staff, and the ability of the staff to communicate with and understand the client. Intake procedures may involve a series of psychological tests for evaluating the client's condition which requires several visits, may be limited to an admissions interview, or may be included as part of an interview therapy session in the case of adaptive assistance. Similarly, the length of admissions forms and whether they are self-administered or the information is secured through an interview will tend to influence the client's response to the service. Each of these characteristics may convey a frustrating sense of dealing with a bureaucracy. When intake requires several visits, many patients will find the investment in effort unattractively costly, especially those clients who are ambivilant toward therapy and have a short time horizon.[11] Waiting time to be admitted to therapy, which in some instances requires two or more weeks after the initial contact with an agency, operates as a cost to the client in a manner similar to the length of intake procedure.

Expertness of the staff is difficult for the clients to objectively evaluate but their judgment, often based on comments by others and superficial observation, will affect the user's valuation of the service.[12] The apparent quality of the therapists and other staff involved in the treatment program will affect both trust and expectations concerning outcome, and personal estimates of the length of treatment or amount of effort that therapy will require. Closely associated with the apparent expertness of personnel is the ability and motivation of staff members to communicate with the clients and to understand their life situations.[13] The differences in class and experiences between professionals and especially lower-income clients have created such a massive barrier to developing effective therapeutic relations that some writers question the appropriateness of interview therapy for the poor.[14] The problems of communication and resulting client alienation are a major argument for employing indigenous nonprofessionals and volunteers to work with clients in intake, some counseling concerning situational problems, and as members of a therapeutic team.[15] Establishing active contact with the community groups and locating the clinic in the community are additional means for the professional to gain an understanding of the life and communication styles of clients.

Community involvement in developing the program objectives and in the administration of the agency further assists the staff in understanding clients and their problems, helps to insure the appropriateness of services that are provided, and through political and social inclusion of the population to be served, encourages community acceptance or "adoption" of the agency.[16] Yet another characteristic of the service is continuity of treatment, both in the sense of integrating several related services so that the client may obtain several kinds of assistance at the same location and such that a client sees the same staff member or therapeutic team at each visit. Continuity of care appears to play a substantial role in consumer satisfaction in allowing the user to develop expectations, and continuity is an item of information which is informally communicated to prospective clients by other members of the community.[17]

A final feature of the service program is the scheduled time at which services are available.[18] When open hours are limited to common business hours, a special problem is posed for employed clients or when an employed member of a family is needed for babysitting. Conflicts between agency hours and a consumer's nondiscretionary hours, coupled with a tendency for emotional problems to be especially acute during the night, are reasons for the popularity of twenty-four hour Crisis Clinic services and nighttime partial hospitalization.[19]

Characteristics of the Facility

A third group of service package features affecting demand for outpatient care relate to the setting in which therapy is provided. Characteristics of the structure housing the service can have important symbolic and psychological impact on consumers. Increasingly, research is adding to our understanding of the ways in which the use of color, space, and textures influence the emotions of individuals and their use of structures.[20] For example, use of big windows and interior decoration with colorful walls and furniture, rather than a purely efficient layout with hospital green and antiseptic white, will tend to encourage utilization.[21] Similarly, pleasing landscaping and outdoor sitting space, along with "symbolically open" design of buildings which are not walled off from the community will positively affect the attitude of residents toward the facility and consequently the service.[22] The scale of the facility also affects response toward an agency. Large facilities are commonly confusing to use and tend to intimidate some prospective clients.[23]

Currently, little is known about the direct effect of characteristics of a facility on consumer demand. Considerable discussion has centered on the role of various features of facility design on attitude toward, and community acceptance of, a service package provided by an agency, which in turn affects utilization.[24] Except in cases in which the facility has the effect of antagonizing or alienating the prospective consumer, features of the service program discussed above appear to have a far greater impact on willingness to seek outpatient service at an agency than does the design of the structure accommodating that agency.

Relative Location of the Facility

The fourth group of service package characteristics deal with the location of the agency relative to the locations of consumers. The role of accessibility and measures of distance are extensively discussed in Chapter 2. Direct travel cost to reach an agency is a tangible expense to the client in consuming the service, but within a catchment area it does not appear to exert important influences on behavior. Travel time-distance is probably of greater importance in affecting the choice of the agency to use.[25] Where residents have a choice of several agencies at which they may secure comparable services, some agencies may be located in a manner such that they provide "intervening opportunities," or services which, because they are closer, are relatively more attractive.[26]

In addition to distance, travel by persons to an activity location requires knowledge of opportunities for satisfying demand. It appears that a person's activities occur within a field of preestablished contacts, that is, at places which the person has visited and is familiar.[27] This information is in part a product of interpersonal communication which is in turn socially determined. [28] This learning model of spatial behavior suggests the possibility of a substitution between information and physical accessibiltiy of a service in stimulating utilization. It also suggests that localization of the service, placing points of supply within the residential area familiar to the client or in a center frequented by the client, will aid in decreasing access costs based on knowledge, as well as facilitating multiple purpose trips.[29] Similarly, localization could increase residents' acceptance and identity with an agency if this location is part of their residential territory.[30]

An additional characteristic with regard to spatial behavior and the effect of distance is the degree of mobility individuals have as a result of their social roles.[31] Thus a mother with children would tend to be less mobile than a person without a family.

Price of the Service

The price of the service is possibly the most straight forward and most easily treated of the characteristics. When price is subsidized, as is the case for most clients of a community mental health center, it may play a relatively insignificant role in influencing demand. An income-based fee schedule, with the balance of the direct cost borne by government funding programs, is intended to increase the consumption of the particular service by decreasing the relative cost to the consumer. The fee schedule may be manipulated to account for income differences in the marginal value of money and to favor groups of the population who might commonly have more reticence in using a service or proportionately greater incidence of disability.

It appears, however, that price manipulation has limited value as a technique for effectively encouraging consumption of mental health services by the psychiatrically disabled. Free provision of service to the poor, for example, has enabled and encouraged these individuals to consume the service, but revealed demand appears to continually account for only a fraction of total demand. One interpretation of this situation is that the people whose demand remains latent face costs other than the fees charged, or services which yield too low a level of satisfaction, for direct net benefits to be adequately positive to result in utilization. Thus to secure utilization by every mentally disabled resident through price manipulation, for example, would probably require negative pricing or payments to the users. Such a tactic would be difficult to administer and is probably politically unacceptable. Alternatively, use might be subsidized and required of the mentally ill, much as public school attendance is required of children. This is the current practice for cases in which the individual is acutely ill and dangerous, but the resulting infringement of personal freedom makes this an even less acceptable tactic than direct payments to clients for using the service.

While price is conventionally the most important variable in demand analysis, its role in affecting behavior with respect to psychiatric care is complicated by two relatively unusual features of mental health services. First, because of consumer ignorance in evaluating therapy and the services provided by alternative suppliers, prices are widely used as an indicator of quality.[32] For example, a higher-priced service may be preferred over an equally effective but less expensive one based on the presumption that it must be better. This may be a major reason behind the general preference for individual therapy over group therapy. The same pattern of reasoning appears to operate when people evaluate the probable quality of the service which they are receiving on the basis of the professional training of therapists or the furnishings and building of the agency. The tendency to evaluate quality by price, or cost, might be offset by providing reliable information including alternative indices which consumers could use in judging the value of alternative services.

Secondly, therapists have traditionally used prices as a means of securing a client's commitment to the treatment program. It is reasoned that if the consumer is required to give up something of personal value for therapy, that the therapy sessions will be taken seriously and used intensively. The price charged is the easiest means of access a supplier has to a consumer's resources in this case. Other means of securing commitment such as the nature of the therapist-client relationship of the prospect of successful treatment must be substituted at least in part for price when the service is provided on a subsidized basis.[33]

To summarize, it is expected that the elasticity of demand with respect to price would be high, especially for a service which is unfamiliar to prospective clients and uncertain in its results. Reduction in price through subsidies has had the anticipated affect of increasing consumption of outpatient care, but has failed to motivate all of the psychiatrically disabled in the population to seek therapy. Where the purpose is to induce effective utilization of the service, price manipulation must be accompanied by modification of other characteristics of the good; characteristics relating to the availability, accessibility, and acceptability of the service.

A Consumer Response Model for Mental Health Services

The selected characteristics of mental health services discussed in the last section may be used in formulating a model of consumer response to various ways in which outpatient care is provided. As will be apparent, problems with specification of several of the variables involved and with availability of data for other variables currently make this formulation more a guide to research than a method for direct application in planning. The functional representation of this model is adapted from the abstract transportation mode model cited earlier.[34]

If Q_{ij} denotes the demand for outpatient services by the population of area i from agency j, the general form of the model is,

$$Q_{ij} = f(P_i, X_i, W_j), \qquad (9.1)$$

where P_i is the population of area i, X_i denotes other demographic variables of that population, and W_j represents various characteristics of the service delivered by agency j. A more general formulation of the demand equation recognizes the interdependence of a consumer's choice to use one service on the availability of alternative sources of the same or similar types of service. The services of alternative supplying agencies are typified by their various features including: attributes of the client groups using that agency D_j, accessibility of the agency A_{ij}, characteristics of the service provided S_j, mode of therapy available at an agency M_j, features of the facility F_j, and price of the service C_j.[b] Equation (9.1) may then be rewritten as,

$$Q_{ij} = f(P_i, X_i, D, A, S, M, F, C),$$

where D, A, S, M, F, and C are functions of the respective characteristics of the

---

[b]Several of these independent variables denote bundles of characteristics of the service package provided by an agency. Thus these variables represent subfunctions accounting for their various components which, in turn, effect consumer responses. By way of an example, S_j could include for a particular agency the average number of days required on a waiting list, a score for the apparent expertness of the staff, the number of local paraprofessionals

service package as provided by available outpatient clinics. Thus, with respect to accessibility, for example, $A = g(A_{i1}, A_{i2}, \ldots, A_{in})$, where n is the number of alternative agencies or sources providing the service to residents of area i.

The dependent variable, Q_{ij}, may take at least two forms. It may be defined as the number of persons admitted to service, that is, the incidence of treated psychiatric disability from area i treated at agency j. Alternatively, it may be the number of client visits to an agency from an area. Because a center once chosen tends to continue to be the one utilized, and because the number of visits is dependent on characteristics of the individual's disability, the former definition is preferred.

The independent variable for population of the residential subdivision of the catchment served by a cneter, P_i, is expected to have an increasing effect on demand for service. This is the population at risk and operates to standardize the observed or expected use. The relevant location of clients or prospective users might account for places of employment or other day-time distribution, but the assumption here is that place of residence is the more important referent. In the empirical work reported in preceeding chapters, frequency of first admissions from residential areas during sample months were standardized for variation in the population size of these various areas. Thus population size was accounted for on the left-hand side of the equation, and therefore did not appear among the variables on the right.

Effort is commonly made to include general demographic characteristics of a population residing in various portions of a service area, as approximations of client descriptions, in exploring variations in demand. It is even more desirable to typify actual consumers of a service by their demographic characteristics, data which is often unavailable for demand studies. Income, race, diagnosis or severity of condition, and occupation are especially useful characteristics. Analysis of consumer data reported earlier in this study separately examined the behavior of client groups defined on the basis of these and other characteristics.

Borrowing further from the model of consumer responses developed by Quandt and Baumol,[35] an elaborated version of equation (9.2) may be stated as,

$$Q_{ij} = a_0 \, P_i^{a_1} \, D_i^{a_2} \, N_i^{a_3} \, f_1(S) f_2(F) f_3(A) \ldots f_m(C) \qquad (9.3)$$

where, for example

$$f_3(A) = (A^b)^{g_1} (A_j^r)^{g_2}.$$

working with the agency, and so forth. Data availability and computational complexity could require substituting simple composites of scores on these specific characteristics for the subfunctions mentioned above. While this would limit evaluation of the contribution to demand of these characteristics, this tactic could direct additional research attention to a select number of major factors influencing utilization. Alternatively, successive regression of a limited number of specific variables on consumer behavior could be used to identify their statistical value in explaining variation.

The variables are as defined and discussed above, with additional notations including:

N_i = number of agencies or sources of supply of outpatient care available to the population of area i;

b = superscript denoting the value of the best available service with respect to a particular variable, for example A_i^b is the time-distance of the closest agency to area i;

r = superscript denoting the relative value of a service provided by a particular agency with respect to the associated variable, for example, A_{ij}^r is the time-distance of agency j from area i divided by the least time-distance, A^b.

The subfunctions such as the one given in the example above may be individually analyzed. Data collected through survey research could be used to establish which agency is considered best with respect to the specific characteristic of the service program and how individuals regard the several criteria defining the character of the service package provided by various agencies.

The coefficients in equation (9.3) take the form of exponential values to express interdependence among the factors influencing demand, and this also permits the function to be loglinearized. Several factors in this function require further comment. Demographic features of the population of an area, D_i, may be omitted if the function is used separately for each demographic group residing in i. In this case, P_i would refer to the population residing in i with the particular demographic characteristics.

Alternatively, Q_{ij} could be expressed as first admissions of patients with a particular set of demographic characteristics from i to j, divided by the population in i with these characteristics. Then P_i would not appear on the right-hand side of the equation. A variation on this approach was used in the analysis of client data reported in earlier chapters of this study. Finally, the number of alternative sources of service available to residents of an area, N_{ij}, is redundant and may be deleted if all areas in a catchment being analyzed may obtain service at all agencies.[c]

Further analysis identified several weaknesses in this formulation, including the unresponsiveness of demand to changes in agencies other than the particular agency j or the "best" agency with respect to the specific criteria used.[36] Applying theory developed by Mayberry [37] which further stipulated the form of the function, equation (9.3) may be rewritten as,

$$Q_{ij} = a_0 \, P_i^{a_1} \, G_{ij} \left(\sum_k G_{ij} \right)^{a-1}, \qquad 0 < a < 1^{38} \tag{9.4}$$

---

[c]Quandt and Baumol note that N has the disadvantage of suggesting a role for "irrelevant alternatives" in influencing demand.[39]

where $G_{ij} = S_j^{a_2} M_j^{a_3} F_j^{a_4} C_j^{a_5} D_j^{a_6} A_{ij}^{a_7}$,

and each of the independent variables in the subfunction have the interpretation stated above.

This function states that demand for service by a subpopulation from an agency is not only dependent on characteristics of the service provided by the agency, but on the counterpart characteristics of all services which could be substituted by that population.

A number of alternative forms of such a function for transportation demand were developed and extensively tested by Quandt and Young.[40] Adaptation of a formulation which they found most successful leads to rewriting (9.3) and (9.4) as,

$$\ln Q_{ij} = a_0 P_i^{a_1} (S_j^r)^{a_2} (M_j^r)^{a_3} (F_j^r)^{a_4} (C_j^r)^{a_5} (D_j^r)^{a_6} (A_{ij}^r)^{a_7} e^{a_8}. \quad (9.5)$$

This function has theoretical support both from empirical work reported in preceding chapters and the work of authors cited in this chapter. This formulation also has some record of success in tests using transportation data as reported by Quandt and Young, and substantial logical appeal as a model of consumer decision-making where a number of supply characteristics are influential and are interdependent in their effect. As pointed out in Chapter 2, a function with a similar form recently has been used in health services research for analyzing flows of patients from residential areas to hospitals.[41]

A model of the sort developed in this chapter is heuristically useful to gaining an understanding of consumer responses to the way in which a service such as outpatient mental health care is provided. Furthermore, such a model could provide a basis for testing theories concerning consumer behavior, through comparing simulation results with empirical observations. As analysis of client data reported in this study points up, however, we have just begun to identify and to specify variables which realistically typify the way in which a service is supplied. Similarly, we have only begun to deal with differences in the behavior of various client groups in response to these supply variables. Consequently, a great deal of empirical work remains to be done in developing a coherent and systematic body of consumer behavior theory which deals with urban public services. Availability of such theory is a requisite for designing services which are effective from the consumers' perspective; if, in other words, we are to gain a sound analytical basis for user-oriented planning.

Notes

Notes to Chapter 2
Consumer Behavior in Selecting and Utilizing Health Services
Theoretical and Empirical Studies

1. John L. Hancock, "Planners in the Changing American City, 1900-1940," *Journal of the American Institute of Planners* 33 (September 1967): 290-304; Frederick Law Olmsted, "Introduction," in John Nolen (ed.), *City Planning* (New York: D. Appleton and Company, 1916), pp. 1-15; Mel Scott, *American City Planning Since 1890* (Berkeley: University of California Press, 1969).

2. Martin Rein, "Social Planning: The Search for Legitimacy," *Journal of the American Institute of Planners* 35 (July 1969): 233-44; Paul Davidoff and Thomas A. Reiner, "A Choice Theory of Planning," *Journal of the American Institute of Planners* 28 (May 1962): 103-115; Albert Z. Guttenberg, "Urban Structure and Urban Growth," *Journal of the American Institute of Planners* 26 (May 1960): 104-110. Frieden suggests that the planning profession has successively emphasized responsiveness and social concern at its beginnings around the turn of the century, during the 1930s, and beginning again in the early 1960s. Bernard J. Frieden, "The Changing Prospects for Social Planning," *Journal of the American Institute of Planners* 33 (September 1967): 311-23.

3. Nelson N. Foote, "Community Services," *The Annals of the American Academy of Political and Social Sciences* 314 (November 1957): 46-56; Melvin M. Webber, "Comprehensive Planning and Social Responsibility: Toward an AIP Consensus on the Profession's Roles and Purposes," *Journal of the American Institute of Planners* 39 (November 1963): 232-41.

4. Janet S. Reiner, Everett Reimer, and Thomas A. Reiner, "Client Analysis and the Planning of Public Programs," *Journal of the American Institute of Planners* 39 (November 1963): 270-82; Lisa R. Peattie, "Reflections on Advocacy Planning," *Journal of the American Institute of Planners* 34 (March 1968): 80-88.

5. Susan and Norman Fainstein, "City Planning and Political Views," *Urban Affairs Quarterly* 6 (March 1971): 341-362; Michael P. Brooks, *Social Planning and City Planning* (Chicago: American Society of Planning Officials, 1970), pp. 33-38: Herbert J. Gans, *People and Plans* (New York: Basic Books 1968), pp. 71-75; Leo Jacobson, "Toward a Pluralistic Ideology in Planning Education," in Ernest Erber (ed.), *Urban Planning in Transition* (New York: Grossman Publishers, 1970), pp. 266-75.

6. Gans, *People and Plans*, p. 53.

7. John W. Dyckman et.al., "Community Facilities: Social Values and

Goals in Planning for Education, Health, and Recreation" (Berkeley: Institute of Urban and Regional Development, University of California, 1967). (Mimeographed.)

8. Gans, *People and Plans,* p. 55.

9. Ibid., pp. 54-55.

10. Ibid., p. 97.

11. Ibid., p. 96.

12. Ibid., p. 104.

13. Bernard J. Frieden and James Peters, "Urban planning and Health Services: Opportunities for Cooperation," *Journal of the American Institute of Planners* 36 (March 1970): 82-95.

14. See, for example, Surgeon General's Ad Hoc Committee on Planning for Mental Health Facilities, *Planning of Facilities for Mental Health Services,* Public Health Service Publication No. 808. (Washington: U.S. Department of Health, Education, and Welfare, Public Health Service, January 1961), pp. 3-4, 13, 31.

15. Michael B. Teitz, *Toward a Theory of Urban Public Facility Location,* Center for Planning and Development Research Working Paper No. 67 (Berkeley: The Center, 1967), pp. 7-11.

16. Ibid., pp. 17-18. See also, William Baumol and Edward Ide, "Variety in Retailing," *Management Science* 3 (October 1956): 93-101.

17 Allan Blackman, "The Meaning and Use of Standards," in Henrik L. Blum and Associates, *Health Planning* (Berkeley: Comprehensive Health Planning Unit, School of Public Health, University of California, 1969), pp. 4.33-4.39, and Thomas M. Dunaye, "Hospital Service Area Planning and Patient Origin Analysis," in *Methods of Estimating Hospital Bed Needs* (Los Angeles: School of Public Health, University of California, October, 1967), pp. VIII–1-VIII–24. For examples, see: National Commission on Community Health Services, *Health is a Community Affair* (Cambridge: Harvard University Press, 1966); American Public Health Association, *Guide to a Community Health Study* (New York: The Association, 1961); Sven Godlund, *Population, Regional Hospitals, Transport Facilities, and Regions: Planning the Location of Regional Hospitals in Sweden,* Lund Studies in Geography, Series B: Human Geography, No. 21 (Lund: The Royal University of Lund, Department of Geography, 1961); A.J. Januard and R. Lachene, "Elaboration du Programme d'Equipment d'un Hospital, Cas du Centre Hospitalier et Universitaire de Rennes," *Revue Metra* 3 (1964): 207-218.

18. Blackman, "Standards." Also see Dyckman et al., *Community Facilities,* pp. 4-8.

19. Robert E. Coughlin, "Hospital Complex Analysis: An Approach to Analysis for Planning a Metropolitan System of Service Facilities," (Ph.D. dissertation, University of Pennsylvania, 1964); Anthony J.S. Rourke, *A Study*

Report to the Lincoln Hospital Council: A Master Plan for Development of Facilities (Lincoln, Nebraska: The Council, 1964).

20. For additional criticisms of the area approach, see Jerry B. Schneider, "A New Approach to Areawide Planning of Metropolitan Hospital Systems," *Hospitals, Journal of the American Hospital Association* 42 (April 16, 1968): 79-83. See also, Richard L. Morrill and Robert Earickson, "Locational Efficiency of Chicago Hospitals: An Experimental Model," *Health Services Research* 4 (Summer 1969): 128-41.

21. C.E. Lively and P.G. Beck, *The Rural Health Facilities of Ross County, Ohio,* Ohio AES Bulletin 412 (Wooster: Ohio Agricultural Extension Service, October 1927).

22. Isabella C. Wilson and William H. Metzler, *Sickness and Medical Care in an Ozark Area in Arkansas,* Arkansas AES Bulletin 353 (Fayetteville: Arkansas Agricultural Extension Service, April 1938). Also, T.C. McCormick, *Rural Social Organization in South Central Arkansas,* Arkansas AES Bulletin 313 (Fayetteville: Arkansas Agricultural Extension Service, December 1934), p. 29.

23. Paul J. Jehlik and Robert L. McNamara, "The Relation of Distance to the Differential Use of Certain Health Personnel and Facilities and to the Extent of Bed Illness," *Rural Sociology* 17 (1952): 261-65.

24. A. Ciocco and I. Altman, *Medical Service Areas and Distances Travelled for Physician Care in Western Pennsylvania,* Public Health Monograph No. 19 (Washington: U.S. Department of Health, Education, and Welfare, Public Health Service, 1954).

25. James E. Weiss, "The Effect of Medical Centers on the Distribution of Physicians in the United States," (Ph.D. dissertation. University of Michigan, 1968). Also see Stanley W. Lieberson, "Ethnic Groups and the Practice of Medicine," *American Sociological Review* 23 (October 1958): 542-48.

26. Morrill and Earickson, "Locational Efficiency," p. 131.

27. R.G. Golledge, "Conceptualizing the Market Decision Process," *Journal of Regional Science* 7 (Winter 1967): 239-58. This concept has been applied, in other terms, in delimiting a set of service areas for several urban hospitals. Rourke, "Report to the Lincoln Hospital Council."

28. James E. Weiss, Merwyn R. Greenlick and Joseph F. Jones, "Determinants of Medical Care Utilization: The Impact of Ecological Factors," Paper presented at the 98th Annual Meeting of the American Public Health Association, Houston, Texas, October 1970. (Mimeographed.)

29. Ibid., p. 11.

30. Jerry B. Schneider, "Measuring, Evaluating and Redesigning Hospital-Patient-Physician Spatial Relationships in Metropolitan Areas," *Inquiry* 5 (June 1968): 24-43. Also see, Jerry B. Schneider, "Measuring the Locational Efficiency of the Urban Hospital," *Health Services Research* 2 (Summer 1967): 154-169.

31. Richard Morrill and William Garrison, "Highways and Services: The Case of Physician Care," in W.L. Garrison et al., *Studies of Highway Development and Geographic Change* (Seattle: University of Washington Press, 1959), pp. 227-76.

32. Ibid., p. 241.

33. Richard L. Morrill and Robert Earickson, "Hospital Variation and Patient Travel Distances," *Inquiry* 5 (December 1968): 26-34. For similar findings, see A. Mizrahi, A. Mizrahi and G. Rosch, "Les Champs d'Action des Equipments Hospitaliers," *Consommation* 10 (July-September 1963): 60-106.

34. Morrill and Earickson, "Locational Efficiency," p. 134.

35. H.D. Cherniack and J.B. Schneider, *A New Approach to the Delineation of Hospital Service Areas,* Regional Science Research Institute Discussion Paper No. 16 (Philadelphia: The Institute, August 1967).

36. Schneider, "Measuring the Locational Efficiency," pp. 154-55, 164; Ira S. Lowry, "Location Parameters in the Pittsburgh Model," *Papers of the Regional Science Association* 11 (1963): 145-65.

37. Schneider, "Measuring . . . Spatial Relationships in Metropolitan Areas."

38. Coughlin, "Hospital Complex Analysis"; Robert E. Coughlin, Walter Isard, and Jerry B. Schneider, *The Activity Structure and Transportation Requirements of a Major University Hospital,* Regional Science Research Institute Discussion Paper No. 4 (Philadelphia: The Institute, 1964).

39. Robert Earickson, "A Behavioral Approach to Spatial Interaction: The Case of Physician and Hospital Care," (Ph.D. dissertation, University of Washington, 1968).

40. Gary W. Shannon, Rashid L. Bashshur, and Charles A. Metzner, "The Concept of Distance as a Factor in Accessibility and Utilization of Health Care," *Medical Care Review* 26 (February 1969): 143-61.

41. Godlund, *Population, Regional Hospitals.*

42. Joint Committee of the American Hospital Association and U.S. Public Health Service, *Areawide Planning for Hospitals and Related Health Facilities,* PHS Publication No. 855 (Washington: GPO, July, 1961). A study of plans for health services notes that while accessbility is an appropriate goal, it was not mentioned in the reports surveyed. Frieden and Peters, "Urban Planning," p. 87.

43. Philip B. Hallen, "Hospitals Branch-Out: A Study of Multiple-Unit Operations, Part I," *Hospitals, Journal of the American Hospital Association* 34 (August 1, 1963): 38-44, 132. W. Wilson Turner, "'Satellite' Hospitals Bring Health Care to Suburbanites," *Modern Hospital* 99 (November 1962).

44. Ralph Morrinson, "Hospital Service Areas: Time Replaces Space," *Hospitals, Journal of the American Hospital Association* 38 (January 16, 1964): 52-54.

45. Ibid.

46. Michael A. Stegman reports similar findings for large metropolitan areas in "Accessibility Models and Residential Location," *Journal of the American Institute of Planners* 35 (January 1969): 22-29.

47. Daniel L. Drosness, Jerome W. Lubin, and Larry G. Wylie, "Highway Network Minimum Path Selection Applied to Health Facility Planning," *Public Health Reports* 80 (September 1965): 771-78.

48. Daniel L. Drosness and Jerome W. Lubin, "Planning Can Be Based on Patient Travel," *The Modern Hospital* 106 (April 1966): 92-94.

49. Ibid., p. 2.

50. Ibid., p. 276. 51.

51. Shannon et al., "Concepts of Distance," p. 155.

52. Ibid., p. 147.

53. Torstein Hägerstrand, "What About People in Regional Science," *Papers of the Regional Science Association* 24 (1970): 7-21. See also, Stanford M. Lyman and Marvin B. Scoff, "Territoriality: A Neglected Sociological Dimension," *Social Problems* 15 (1967): 236-49.

54. Julian Wolpert, "The Decision Process in a Spatial Context," *Annals of the Association of American Geographers* 45 (1964): 537-58; Peter R. Gould, *On Mental Maps*, Michigan Inter-University Community of Mathematical Geographers Discussion Paper No. 9 (Ann Arbor: University of Michigan, 1966); Allan Pred, *Behavior and Location: Foundations for a Geographic and Dynamic Location Theory*, Lund Studies in Geography, Series B: Human Geography, No. 27 (Lund: The Royal University of Lund, Department of Geography, 1967); Gerald Rushton, "Analysis of Spatial Behavior by Revealed Space Preference," *Annals, Association of American Geographers* 59 (1969): 391-400.

55. Earickson, "Behavioral Approach to Spatial Interaction," p. 15. See also Walter Isard, *Location and Space Economy* (Cambridge: M.I.T. Press, 1960), pp. 84-85.

56. Roger M. Downs, "The Cognitive Structure of an Urban Shopping Center," *Environment and Behavior* (June 1970): 13-39.

57. Julian Wolpert, "Behavioral Aspects of the Decision to Migrate," *Papers of the Regional Science Association* 15 (1965): 159-69.

58. Frank E. Horton and David R. Reynolds, "An Investigation of Individual Action Spaces: A Progress Report, *Proceedings, Association of American Geographers* 1 (1969): 70-75. See also, Herbert A. Simon, "Rational Choice and the Structure of the Environment," *Psychological Review* 63 (1956): 129-38.

59. Kurt Lewin, *Field Theory in Social Science* (New York: Harper and Brothers, 1951), p. 246; Richard L. Meier, "Measuring Social and Cultural Change in Urban Regions," *Journal of the American Institute of Planners* 25

(1959): 180-90; Edward T. Hall, *The Hidden Dimension* (Garden City: Doubleday, 1966).

60. Leon Festinger, Stanley Schacter, and Kurt Black, *Social Pressures in Informal Groups* (New York: Harper and Brothers, 1950); Albert H. Rubenstein and Chadwich J. Haberstrol, *Some Theories of Organization* (Homewood, Illinois: Richard D. Irwin, Inc. and the Dorsey Press, 1964); Gould, *On Mental Maps*, p. 8; John B. Lansing and Gary Hendricks, *Automobile Ownership and Residential Density* (Ann Arbor: University of Michigan Survey Research Center, Institute for Social Research, 1967), pp. 57-68; Robert Sommer, "Man's Proximate Environment," *Journal of Social Issues* 22 (1966): 59-70. Joseph Sonnenfeld, "Personality and Behavior in Environment," *Proceedings, Association of American Geographer* 1 (1969): 136-40.

61. See, for example, Suzanne Keller, "Neighborhood Concepts in Sociological Perspective," *Ekistics* 22 (1966): 67-76.

62. J. Smith and F.L. Maddox, "The Spatial Location and Use of Selected Facilities in a Middle-Sized City," *Social Forces* 38 (1959-1960): 119-24.

63. F. Stuart Chapin and Henry C. Hightower, *Household Activity Systems: A Pilot Investigation* (Chapel Hill: University of North Carolina, Center for Urban and Regional Studies, 1966).

64. Theodore Caplow, "The Definition and Measurement of Ambiences," *Social Forces* 34 (1955-1956): 28-33.

65. Morrill and Earickson, "Hospital Variation."

66. Roslyn Lindheim, "Develop Health Facilities Where People Congregate," *California Health* 24 (August 1966): 35-38.

67. Guido Crocetti, Herzl Spiro, and Iradj Siassi, "Are the Ranks Closed? Attitudinal Social Distance and Mental Illness," *American Journal of Psychiatry* 127 (March 1971): 41-47.

68. Earickson, "Behavioral Approach to Spatial Interaction."

69. Ibid., p. 18.

70. See, for example, Gerald D. Suttles, *The Social Order of the Slum* (Chicago: University of Chicago Press, 1968).

71. Earickson, "Behavioral Approach to Spatial Interaction," pp. 23-29.

72. Ibid., p. 38.

73. Ibid., pp. 102-105.

74. For a thorough review of the extensive literature in quantitative geography on gravity models, see Gunnar Olsson, *Distance and Human Interaction: A Review and Bibliography,* Regional Science Research Institute Bibliography Series No. 2 (Philadelphia: The Institute, 1965).

75. Samuel A. Stouffer, "Intervening Opportunities: A Theory Relating Mobility and Distance," *American Sociological Review* 5 (1940): 845-67;

Samuel A. Stouffer, "Intervening Opportunities and Competing Migrants," *Journal of Regional Science* 2 (1960): 1-26.

76. Morrill and Earickson, "Locational Efficiency," p. 129.

77. Richard L. Morrill and Robert Earickson, "Variation in the Character and Use of Chicago Area Hospitals," *Health Services Research* 3 (Fall 1968): 224-38.

78. Ibid., p. 236.

79. Cherniack and Schneider, *Delineation of Hospital Service Areas.*

80. Schneider, "Measuring the Locational Efficiency," pp. 162-63.

81. Paul J. Feldstein, "Research on the Demand for Health Services," *Milbank Memorial Fund Quarterly* 44 (July 1966): 128-62.

82. See for example, Richard L. Morrill and Philip Rees, *Physician Referral and Patient to Hospital Flows,* Chicago Regional Hospital Study Working Paper I.11 (Chicago: The Study, 1967).

83. Feldstein, "Demand for Health Services," p. 155.

84. Kong-Kyun Ro, "Patient Characteristics, Hospital Characteristics and Hospital Use," *Medical Care,* 7 (July-August, 1969), 295-312.

85. Feldstein, "Demand for Health Services," p. 138.

86. Cherniack and Schneider, *Delineation of Hospital Service Areas.*

87. "Behavioral Approach to Spatial Interaction," pp. 67, 69.

88. Morrill and Earickson, "Character and Use of Chicago Area Hospitals," p. 236.

89. Morrill and Earickson, "Locational Efficiency," p. 134.

90. Schneider, "Measuring the Locational Efficiency," pp. 165-66.

91. Peter Cowan, "Hospital Systems and Systems of Hospitals," *Transactions of the Bartlett Society* 5 (1966-1967): 103-122.

92. Morrinson, "Hospital Service Areas"; Godlund, *Population, Regional Hospitals.*

93. Cherniack and Schneider, *Delineation of Hospital Service Areas.*

94. Douglas B. Lee, *Analysis and Description of Residential Segregation* (Ithaca: Cornell University Division of Urban Studies, Center for Housing and Environmental Studies, 1966).

95. Cherniack and Schneider, *Delineation of Hospital Service Areas.*

96. See, Harold W. Kuhn and Robert E. Kuenne, "An Efficient Algorithm for the Numerical Solution of the Generalized Weber Problem in Spatial Economics," *Journal of Regional Science* 4:2 (Winter 1962): 21-33.

97. For a discussion and extensive bibliography, see, Roberto Bachi, "Standard Distance Measures and Related Methods for Spatial Analysis," *Papers, Regional Science Association* 10 (1963): 83-132.

98. Schneider, "Areawide Planning of Metropolitan Hospital Systems."

99. Rashid L. Bashshur, Gary W. Shannon, and Charles A. Metzner, "The Applications of Three-Dimensional Analogue Models to the Distribution of Medical Care Facilities," *Medical Care* 8 (September-October, 1970): 395-407.

100. Ibid., p. 402.

101. Pierre de Visé *"Methods and Concepts of an Interdisciplinary Regional Hospital Study," Health Services Research* 3 (Fall 1968): 166-73.

102. Frieden and Peters, "Urban Planning," pp. 88, 93.

103. Jerry A. Solon, Cecil G. Sheps, and Sidney S. Lee, "Delineating Patterns of Medical Care," *American Journal of Public Health* 50 (August 1960): 1105-1113.

104. Jerry A. Solon, "Patterns of Medical Care: Sociocultural Variables Among a Hospital's Outpatients," *American Journal of Public Health* 56 (June 1966): 884-94. See also, Edward A. Suchman, "Social Patterns of Illness and Medical Care," *Journal of Health and Human Behavior* 6 (Spring 1965): 2-16.

105. Jerry Alan Solon, "Outpatient Care: A Term in Search of a Concept," *Hospitals, Journal of the American Hospital Association* 39 (March 1965): 61-65.

106. Solon, "Patterns of Medical Care."

107. "Behavioral Approach to Spatial Interaction," pp. 36, 38.

108. Saxon Graham, "Social Factors in Relation to the Chronic Illnesses," in H.E. Freeman (ed.), *Handbook of Medical Sociology* (Englewood Cliffs, N.J.: Prentice-Hall, 1963); and Lieberson, "Ethnic Groups and the Practice of Medicine."

109. Pierre de Visé, *Slum Medicine, Chicago Style: How the Medical Needs of the City's Negro Poor are Met,* Chicago Regional Hospital Study Working Paper IV.8 (Chicago: The Study, 1968).

110 Morrill and Earickson, "Locational Efficiency," p. 129. See also, Morrill and Earickson, "Character and Use of Chicago Area Hospitals," p. 236.

111. Morrill and Earickson, "Locational Efficiency," p.133.

112. Ibid., p. 134.

113. Louis Kriesberg, "The Relationship between Socio-Economic Rank and Behavior," *Social Problems* 49 (1963): 334-53; Feldstein, "Demand for Health Services," pp. 146-52; Ro, "Patient Characteristics," pp. 297, 303, 305, 309; Charlotte Muller, "Income and the Receipt of Medical Care," *American Journal of Public Health* 55 (April 1965): 510-521; U.S. Department of Health, Education, and Welfare, *Selected Health Characteristics by Occupation,* National Center for Health Statistics, Series 10, No. 21 (Washington: GPO 1965); A. Mizrahi, "Un Modele des Depense Medicales," *Consommation* 12:1 (January-March, 1965): 60-75.

114. Morrill and Garrison, "Highways and Services," p. 244; Richard M. Bailey, "The Microeconomics of Health," in Blum and Associates, *Health Planning* pp. 10.01-10.31. Reviewing much of the literature on this topic, Feldstein concludes that families with higher incomes have higher expenditures, but that the percentage of income spent on health care decreases with higher income levels; that the income elasticity is less than one. "Demand for Health Services," p. 148.

115. Samuel W. Bloom, *The Doctor and His Patient: A Sociological Interpretation* (New York: Russell Sage Foundation, 1963); Muller, "Income and the Receipt of Medical Care," p. 520.

116. Ro, "Patient Characteristics"; Morrill and Garrison, "Highways and Services."

117. Solon, "Patterns of Medical Care," pp. 887-88.

118. Rashid L. Bashshur, Gary W. Shannon, and Charles A. Metzner, "Some Ecological Differences in the Use of Medical Services," Paper presented at the Annual Meeting of the American Sociological Association, Washington, D.C., 1970. (Mimeographed.)

119. Weiss, Greenlick, and Jones, "Determinants of Medical Care Utilization," p. 13.

120. Morrill and Earickson, "Character and Use of Chicago Area Hospitals," p. 236. See also, Richard L. Morrill and Robert Earickson, *Influence of Race, Religion and Ability to Pay on Patient to Hospital Distance*, Chicago Regional Hospital Study Working Paper I.17 (Chicago: The Study, 1968).

121. "Demand for Health Services," pp. 143-44. Also see, Pierre de Visé, *Predicting Pediatric and Geriatric Population Needs of New Life Communities*, Chicago Regional Hospital Study Working Paper III.6 (Chicago: The Study, 1968).

122. "Patient Characteristics," p. 304.

123. "Patterns of Medical Care," p. 887.

124. Feldstein, "Demand for Health Services."

125. "Patient Characteristics."

126. Lansing and Hendricks, *Automobile Ownership,* p. 106.

127. Wolpert,"Behavioral Aspects of the Decision to Migrate," p. 165.

128. Weiss, Greenlick, and Jones "Determinants of Medical Care Utilization," pp. 12-13.

129. "Character and Use of Chicago Area Hospitals," pp. 236-37.

130. "Measuring the Locational Efficiency," p. 167.

131. Ibid.

132. Ro, "Patient Characteristics," p. 297.

133. Earickson, "Behavioral Approach to Spatial Interaction," pp. 93-95.

134. Morrill and Earickson, "Character and Use of Chicago Area Hospitals," pp. 227-29.

135. Morrill and Earickson, "Locational Efficiency," pp. 129, 131. See also, M.S. Goldstein and T.D. Woolsey, *Distance Traveled for Hospital Care in Saskatchewan, 1951* (Washington: U.S. Public Health Service, 1956).

136. Morrill and Earickson, "Character and Use of Chicago Area Hospitals," pp. 236-37. Earickson also uses the number of hospital staff doctors as an index of size ("Behavioral Approach to Spatial Interaction," pp. 87-89).

137. Morrill and Earickson, "Hospital Variation," pp. 32-33.

138. Coughlin, Isard, and Schneider, *Activity Structure . . . of a Major University Hospital.*

139. Mizrahi, Mizrahi, and Rosch, "Les Champs d'Action."

140. M.F. Long and P.J. Feldstein, "Economics of Hospital Systems: Peak Loads and Regional Coordination," *American Economic Review* 57 (1967): 119-29.

141. Coughlin, "Hospital Complex Analysis"; Coughlin, Isard, and Schneider, "Activity Structure of a Major University Hospital."

142. Earickson, "Behavioral Approach to Spatial Interaction," pp. 93-95.

143. "Locational Efficiency," p. 131.

144. Feldstein, "Demand for Health Services," p. 134.

145. Morrill and Earickson, "Character and Use of Chicago Area Hospitals," p. 232.

146. Ro, "Patient Characteristics," p. 311. Ro also notes that the occupancy rate is a function of number of beds, and that together they have a positive and significant relationship to the six measures of hospital use which he employed. This suggests that an increase in the supply of beds will result in some increase in hospital use.

147. de Visé, "Interdisciplinary Regional Hospital Study," p. 168. Dealing with outpatient services, Ginzberg points out that the capacity of hospital emergency departments in New York have been expanded in response to direct consumer demand, while ambulatory care services have not. Patients appear to be substituting the former services for the latter, in part because of the nature of insurance coverages. Eli Ginzberg et al., *Urban Health Services: The Case of New York* (New York: Columbia University Press, 1971), p. 6.

148. "Demand for Health Services," pp. 154-55. Feldstein argues against the notion that capacity is a separate factor affecting the level of demand, but that increased bed supply results from current demand or trends in demand. Ibid.

149. "Measuring the Locational Efficiency," p. 168.

150. "Character and Use of Chicago Area Hospitals," p. 237. These authors also note that personnel and payroll are better predictors of capacity or volume

of service than number of beds. Ibid., p. 231. An explanation from Ro's analysis is that staff or service intensive care shortens hospital stays, that this tends to be a distinctive characteristic of larger hospitals, and that patients from higher socio-economic families seem to be attracted to this sort of care. "Patient Characteristics," p. 301. This suggests that, to the extent patients are affected by waiting time, hospitals with high staff to bed ratios would be attractive.

151. "Hospital Variation," pp. 28-29.

152. Morrill and Earickson, "Character and Use of Chicago Area Hospitals," p. 225. Scope of services also includes the availability of outpatient care. Ro notes that, when available, outpatient services appear to be substituted for inpatient care, with the result that the average lenth of stay and expense for hospitalization is reduced. "Patient Characteristics," p. 299.

153. Bailey, "Microeconomics of Health," pp. 10.07-10.08.

154. Jerry B. Schneider, *Measuring the Locational Efficiency of the Urban Hospital,* Regional Science Research Institute Discussion Paper 11 (Philadelphia: The Institute, 1967).

155. "Character and Use of Chicago Area Hospitals," pp. 225-27.

156. Ibid., pp. 236-38.

157. Morrill and Earickson, "Hospital Variation," p. 33.

158. Ibid.

159. Morrill and Earickson, "Locational Efficiency," p. 131.

160. Cherniack and Schneider, *Delineation of Hospital Service Areas.* Of outpatients using clinical services at a large university hospital, 96 percent were found to live less than five miles away. Coughlin, Isard, and Schneider, "Activity Structure of a Major University Hospital."

161. Coughlin, Isard, and Schneider, "Activity Structure of a Major University Hospital." It may be recalled that a patient origin study in Santa Clara County, California, revealed no differences in the attenuating effect of travel time among three major categories of medical services. Drosness and Lubin, "Planning Can Be Based on Patient Travel," p. 93. However, plots of the mean locations of demand by major aggregated groups of medical services for each hospital in Cincinnati demonstrate substantial differences in average distances traveled to the same hospital for different services. See Schneider, "Measuring the Locational Efficiency," pp. 162-63.

162. Hallen, "Hospitals Branch-Out," p. 39.

163. Richard L. Morrill and Robert Earickson, *Hospital Service Areas,* Chicago Regional Hospital Study Working Papers I.5 and I.6 (Chicago: The Study, 1967).

164. Long and Feldstein, "Economics of Hospital Systems."

165. Ginzberg, *Urban Health Services,* p. 7.

166. Ibid., p. 231. Noting the relative isolation of the mental health services, Ginzberg discourages program extensions into areas affecting mental health but not part of psychiatry. Greater effectiveness would result from developing linkages with other systems such as welfare and training programs that can contribute to desired ends. For a report on use of this strategy in a TB control program, see, Francis J. Curry, "Neighborhood Clinics for More Effective Outpatient Treatment of Tuberculosis," (San Francisco: San Francisco Department of Public Health, undated). (Mimeographed.)

167. Francis J. Curry, "A New Approach for Improving Attendence at Tuberculosis Clinics," *American Journal of Public Health* 58:5 (May 1968): 877-81.

168. Miriam Ostow, "TB Control," in Ginzberg, *Urban Health Services,* p. 204.

169. Weiss, Greenlick, and Jones, "Determinants of Medical Care Utilization."

170. Robert L. Nolan et al., "Social Class Differences in Utilization of Pediatric Services in a Prepaid Direct Medical Care Program," *American Journal of Public Health* 57 (1967): 34-47.

171. Pierre de Visé, *Slum Medicine, Chicago Style.*

172. Chicago Commission on Human Relations, *Negro Physicians and Medical Students Affiliated with Chicago Hospitals and Medical Schools* (Chicago: The Commission, 1966).

173. Robert Earickson, *Simulation Model of Nonwhite Hospital Use in Chicago,* Chicago Regional Hospital Study Working Paper III.5 (Chicago: The Study, 1967).

174. Herbert E. Klarman, *The Economics of Health* (New York: Columbia University Press, 1965).

175. Feldstein, "Demand for Health Services," pp. 146-52.

176. Ibid., pp. 146-48. Feldstein notes that even the widely held notion of the price elasticity of medical care being less than one is still an untested hypothesis because of the lack of adequate data.

177. Ro, "Patient Characteristics," p. 301.

178. Ibid., p. 304.

179. Ibid.

180. M.E. Odoroff and L.M. Abbe, "Use of General Hospitals: Variations with Methods of Payment," *Public Health Reports* 74 (April 1959): 316-24. Also see, Paul M. Densen, Eve Balamuth, and Sam Shapiro, *Prepaid Medical Care and Hospital Utilization* (Chicago: The American Hospital Association, 1958); S. Sandier, "L'Influence des Facteurs Economiques sur la Consommation Medicale," *Consommation* 13 (April-June 1966): 71-94.

181. Morrill and Earickson, "Locational Efficiency," p. 133.

182. Ibid., p. 137.

183. Morrill and Earickson, "Character and Use of Chicago Area Hospitals," p. 235

184. Ibid., p. 236.

185. "Demand for Health Services," p. 145.

186. Shannon, Bashshur, and Metzner, "Concept of Distance," p. 153.

187. Morrill and Earickson, "Character and Use of Chicago Area Hospitals," pp. 235-36.

188. Morrill and Earickson, "Locational Efficiency."

189. Ibid., p. 140.

190. Ibid.

Notes to Chapter 3
Community and Mental Health Services

1. David Mechanic, *Mental Health and Social Policy* (Englewood Cliffs, N.J.: Prentice-Hall, 1969), p. 2; Peter Hays, *New Horizons in Psychiatry* (Baltimore: Penguin Books, 1964), p. 9.

2. Erich Fromm, *The Sane Society* (New York: Holt, Rinehart and Winston, 1955).

3. Marie Jahoda, *Current Concepts of Positive Mental Health,* Joint Commission on Mental Health and Illness, Monograph No. 1 (New York: Basic Books, 1958).

4. David P. Ausubel, "Personality Disorder Is Disease," *American Psychologist* 16 (February 1961): 69-74.

5. Thomas S. Szasz, "On the Theory of Psychoanalytic Treatment," *International Journal of Psycho-Analysis* 38 (1957): 166-72.

6. See John A. Clausen, "The Sociology of Mental Health," in R.K. Merton, L. Broom, and L.S. Cottrell, Jr. (eds.), *Sociology Today* (New York: Basic Books, 1959), pp. 485-508.

7. John A. Clausen and Marian R. Yarrow, "The Impact of Mental Illness on the Family," *Journal of Social Issues* 11, no. 4 (1955): 18.

8. Mechanic, *Mental Health,* pp. 18-19.

9. See Gerald Caplan, "Community Psychiatry: Introduction and Overview," in S.E. Goldstone (ed.), *Concepts of Community Psychiatry* (Washington: GPO, 1965), pp. 3-18; R.S. Lazarus, *Psychological Stress and the Coping Process* (New York: McGraw-Hill Book Company, 1966).

10. Mechanic, *Mental Health,* pp. 151-52. Mechanic identifies and discusses five etiological concepts of mental illness. Ibid., Chapter 3.

11. This section is based primarily on John D. Clausen, "Mental Disorders," in Robert Merton and Robert Nisbet (eds.), *Contemporary Social Problems* (New York: Harcourt, Brace and World, 1966), pp. 26-83; and Peter Hays, *New Horizons in Psychiatry,* pp. 10-36.

12. See A. Lewis, "Health as a Social Concept," *British Journal of Sociology* 4 (1953): 109-24.

13. American Psychiatric Association, *Diagnostic and Statistical Manual: Mental Disorders* (Washington: APA, 1952).

14. For a similar definition of medical care, see Paul J. Feldstein, "Research on the Demand for Health Services," *Milbank Memorial Fund Quarterly* 44 (July 1966): 132.

15. A.B. Hollingshead and F. Redlich, *Social Class and Mental Illness* (New York: John Wiley and Sons, 1958), pp. 233-38.

16. *Symposium on Preventive and Social Psychiatry* (Washinton: GPO, 1958), p. 199.

17. S.M. Miller and Elliot G. Mishler, "Social Class, Mental Illness, and American Psychiatry: An Expository Review," *Milbank Memorial Fund Quarterly* 37 (April 1959): 173-99.

18. Miller and Mishler discuss therapist behavior in driving overly demanding patients from treatment by using an unattractive prescription. Ibid., p. 196.

19. For a similar model of the way in which decisions concerning medical services are made, see Feldstein, "Demand for Health Services," p. 139.

20. Phillip Nelson, "Information and Consumer Behavior," *Journal of Political Economy* 78, no. 2 (1970): 311-29; George Katona and Eva Mueller, "A Study of Purchaser Decisions," in Katona and Mueller (eds.), *Consumer Behavior* (New York: New York University Press, 1954), pp. 30-57.

21. Frank A. Sloan, *Planning Public Expenditures on Mental Health Service Delivery,* Rand Report RM-6339-NYC (New York: The New York City Rand Institute, 1971), pp. 3-12.

22. Jacob Feldman, *The Dissemination of Health Information* (Chicago: Aldine Publishing Company, 1966).

23. See Sloan, *Planning Public Expenditures,* p. vi.

24. Ibid.; Miller and Mishler, "Social Class."

25. C.M. Tiebout and D.B. Houston, "Metropolitan Finance Reconsidered: Budget Functions and Multi-Level Governments," *Review of Economics and Statistics* 44, no. 4 (1962): 412-17.

26. Leo Srole et al., *Mental Health in the Metropolis: The Midtown Manhattan Study* (New York: McGraw-Hill, 1962), p. 138.

27. U.S. National Center for Health Statistics, *Medical Care, Health Status and Family Income,* Series 10, No. 9 (Washington:GPO, 1967), p. 7.

28. Thomas S. Langer and Stanley T. Michael, *Life Stress and Mental Health* (New York: Free Press, 1963), pp. 466-67.

29. Srole et al., *Mental Health in the Metropolis*, p. 246.

30. Dorothea Leighton et al., *The Character of Danger* (New York: Basic Books, 1963).

31. Richard J. Plunkett and John E. Gordon, *Epideomiology and Mental Illness*, Joint Commission on Mental Illness and Health, Monograph No. 6 (New York: Basic Books, 1960); Bruce Dohrenwend and Barbara Dohrenwend, "The Problem of Validity in Field Studies of Psychological Disorder," in H. Wechsler et al. (eds.), *Readings in Social Psychological Approaches to Mental Illness* (New York: John Wiley and Sons, 1970).

32. Benjamin Pasamanick, Dean W. Roberts, Paul W. Lemkan, and Dean B. Krueger, "A Survey of Mental Disease in an Urban Population: Prevalence by Race and Income," in F. Riessman, J. Cohen and A. Pearl (eds.), *The Mental Health of the Poor* (New York: Free Press, 1964), pp. 39-48.

33. U.S. Department of Health, Education, and Welfare, Public Health Service, *What is Mental Illness?*, P.H.S. Publication No. 505 (Washington: GPO, 1965). While no fully comparable figures are available for San Francisco, an extensive study of patient records showed 16,354 people received some service from Community Mental Health Service facilities during fiscal 1965-1966. This figure represents 22 out of every 1,000 residents used outpatient facilities some time during the year. J.M. Rogers *An Epidemiological Survey of the Total Patient Population Served by the San Francisco Community Mental Health Services during the Fiscal Year July 1, 1965 through June 30, 1966* (San Francisco: Community Mental Health Services, San Francisco Department of Public Health, 1967), p. 101.

34. U.S. Department of Health, Education, and Welfare, Public Health Service, *Mental Illness and Its Treatment*, P.H.S. Publication No. 1345 (Washington: GPO, 1970).

35. Ibid.

36. Hollinshead and Redlich, "Social Class and Mental Illness."

37. Miller and Mishler, "Social Class."

38. Hollingshead and Redlich, "Social Class and Mental Illness"; John A. Clausen and Melvin L. Kohn, "Relation of Schizophrenia to the Social Structure of a Small City," in Benjamin Pasamanick (ed.), *Epidemiology of Mental Disorder* (Washington: American Association for the Advancement of Science, 1959), pp. 69-94; H.W. Dunham, *Community and Schizophrenia* (Detroit: Wayne State University Press, 1965).

39. R.H. Hardt and S.J. Feinhandler, "Social Class and Mental Hospitalization Prognosis," *American Sociological Review* 24 (December 1959): 815-21; Robert E. Clark, "Psychosis, Income and Occupational Prestige," *American*

Journal of Sociology 54 (March 1949): 433-40; J.N. Morris, "Health and Social Class," *Lancet,* 1 (February 7, 1959): 303-305; Dorothy S. Thomas and Ben Z. Locke, "Marital Status, Education and Occupational Differentials in Mental Disease," *Milbank Memorial Fund Quarterly* 41 (1963): 145-60.

40. See Srole et al., *Mental Health in the Metropolis*; and Rema Lapouse, Mary Monk and Melton Terris, "The Drift Hypothesis in Socio-Economic Differentials in Schizophrenia," *American Journal of Public Health* 46 (August 1956): 978-86.

41. See Paul Barabee and Otto von Maring, "Ethnic Variations in Mental Stress in Families with Psychotic Children," *Social Problems* 1 (October 1953): 48-53; Robert Merton, *Social Theory and Social Structure* (Glencoe: Free Press, 1957), pp. 131-60; and Jacob Tuckman and Robert Kleiner, "Discrepancy Between Aspiration and Achievement as a Predictor of Schizophrenia," *Behavioral Science* 7 (October 1968): 443-47.

42. Dunham, *Community and Schizophrenia,* pp. 190 ff.

43. R.J. Turner, "Social Mobility and Schizophenia," *Journal of Health and Social Behavior* 9 (September 1968): 194-203.

44. For example, see R.J. Turner and M.O. Wagenfeld, "Occupational Mobility and Schizophrenia: An Assessment of the Social Causation and Social Selection Hypothesis," *American Sociological Review* 32 (February 1967): 104-113.

45. J.M. Wanklin, D.F. Fleming, C.W. Buck and G.E. Hobbs, "Factors Influencing the Rate of Admissions to Mental Hospitals," *Journal of Nervous and Mental Disease* 121 (February 1955): 103-116.

46. Hollingshead and Redlich, "Social Class and Mental Illness," pp. 186-89; also Frank Riessman and S.M. Miller, "Social Class and Projective Tests," *Journal of Projective Tests* 22 (December 1958): 432-39.

47. Albert Deutsch, *The Mentally Ill in America* (New York: Columbia University Press, 1949).

48. R.M. Glasscote, D.S. Sanders, H.M. Forstenzer and A.R. Foley, *The Community Mental Health Center* (Washington, D.C.: The Joint Information Service, American Psychiatric Association, 1964), p. 2.

49. Ibid., pp. 4-5.

50. Joint (Congressional) Commission on Mental Illness and Health, *Action for Mental Health* (New York: Basic Books, 1961).

51. National Institute for Mental Health, *Mental Illness and Its Treatment,* Public Health Service Publication No. 1345 (Washington, GPO, 1970), p. 10.

52. Glasscote et al., *Community Mental Health Center,* p. 3.

53. U.S. Department of Health, Education, and Welfare, Public Health Service, *National Institute of Mental Health Support Programs,* P.H.S. Publication No. 1700 (Washington: GPO, 1970), p. 9.

54. Ibid.

55. Mechanic, *Mental Health,* p. 60.

Notes to Chapter 4

Welfare Considerations in the Use of Mental Health
Services

1. For the source and a discussion of these terms, see, Burton A. Weisbrod, "Collective-Consumption Services of Individual-Consumption Goods," *Quarterly Journal of Economics,* 81, no. 3 (1964): 471-77.

2. Paul J. Feldstein, "Research on the Demand for Health Services," *Milbank Memorial Fund Quarterly* 44 (July 1966): 131. See also, Allan Williams, "The Optimal Provision of Public Goods in a System of Local Government," *Journal of Political Economy* 74 (February 1966): 18-33.

3. Julius Margolis, "The Demand for Urban Public Services," in Harvey S. Perloff and Lowdon Wingo, Jr. (eds.), *Issues in Urban Economics* (Baltimore: Johns Hopkins Press, 1968), pp. 527-64.

4. Tibor Scitovsky, "Two Concepts of External Economies," *Journal of Political Economy,* 62, no. 2 (1954): 143-51.

5. For an extensive discussion of external effects of this nature and of the necessary conditions for utility maximization, see James M. Buchanan and William Craig Stubblebine, "Externality," *Economica* N.S. 29, no. 116 (1962): 371-84.

6. P.A. Samuelson, "The Pure Theory of Public Expenditures," *Review of Economics and Statistics* 36, no. 4 (1954): 387-89.

7. Ralph Turvey, "On Divergencies between Social Cost and Private Cost," *Economica,* N.S. 30, no. 119 (1963): 309-13.

8. For one of the most thorough studies of the interpersonal effects of mental illness within a household, see M. Rutter, *Children of Sick Parents: An Environmental and Psychiatric Study* (New York: Oxford University Press, 1966).

9. Samuelson, "Pure Theory"; P.A. Samuelson, "Aspects of Public Expenditure Theories," *Review of Economics and Statistics* 40, no. 4 (1958): 332-38. See also, O.A. Davis and A.B. Whinston, "On the Distinction between Public and Private Goods," *American Economic Review* 57, no. 2 (1967): 360-73.

10. Much of the literature on this phenomenon deals with road congestion. J. Hewitt, "The Calculation of Congestion Taxes on Roads," *Economica* N.S. 31, no. 121 (1964): 72-81; A. Walters, "Theory and Measurement of Private and Social Costs of Highway Congestion," *Econometrica* 39, no. 4 (October 1961): 676-99. See also, Edwin S. Mills, "Some Economic Aspects of Outdoor

Recreation," in Michael J. Brennan (ed.), *Patterns of Market Behavior* (Providence, R.I.: Brown University Press, 1965), pp. 27-42.

11. See, Charles W. Baird, "On the Publicness of Health Care," *Review of Social Economy* 27, no. 2 (1969): 109-119. A similar argument is made in, E. Kalacheck, "Determinants of Teenage Unemployment," *Journal of Human Resources* 4 (Winter 1969): 3-21.

12. Benjamin Pasamanick, Frank Scarpitti, and Simon Dinitz, *Schizophrenics in the Community* (New York: Appleton-Century-Crofts, 1967), pp. 124-125.

13. *Mental Health and Social Policy*, p. 25.

14. See Scitovsky, "Two Concepts"; and David Darwent, *Externality, Agglomeration Economies and City Size,* C.P.D.R. Working Paper No. 109 (Berkeley, Calif.: Center for Planning and Development Research, University of California, 1970).

15. See, for example, Rashi Fein, *The Economics of Mental Health* (New York: Pergamon Press, 1967) pp. 612-35.

16. J. Hoenig and M.W. Hamilton, "The Burden on the Household in an Extramural Psychiatric Service," in H. Freeman and J. Farndale (eds.), *New Aspects of the Mental Health Services* (New York: Pergamon Press, 1967), pp. 612-35.

17. V. Ostrom, C.M. Tiebout and R. Warren, "The Organization of Government in Metropolitan Areas: A Theoretical Inquiry," *American Political Science Review* 55, no. 4 (1961): 831-42; Julius Margolis, "Metropolitan Finance Problems, Territories, Functions and Growth," and Charles M. Tiebout, "An Economic Theory of Fiscal Decentralization," in *Public Finances: Needs, Sources and Utilization,* National Bureau of Economic Research Symposium (Princeton, N.J.: The Bureau, 1961); C.M. Tiebout and D.B. Houston, "Metropolitan Finance Reconsidered"; Allan Williams, "Optimal Provision"; Albert Breton, "A Theory of Government Grants," *Canadian Journal of Economics and Political Science* 31 (1965): 175-87.

18. Kenneth J. Arrow, "Uncertainty and the Welfare Economics of Medical Care," *The American Economic Review* 53 (December 1963): 941-73. A public recognition of uncertainty and a partial form of insurance is the tax deductability of expenditures for mental health care.

19. Ibid., p. 965.

20. Ibid., pp. 961-62.

21. "Collective-Consumption Services."

22. Julius Margolis, "Government in a Market Economy," in *Course Notes: Sixth Short Course in Airport Management* (Berkeley, Calif.: Institute of Transportation and Traffic Engineering, University of California, 1966), pp. 36-37. Even in cases in which an individual is emotionally distressed, assurance to relatives that help is available if it is desired is important in relieving the stress

of a difficult situation. R.S. Lazarus, *Psychological Stress and the Coping Process* (New York: McGraw-Hill Book Company, 1966).

23. "Collective-Consumption Services."

24. Richard Musgrave, *Theory of Public Finance* (New York: McGraw-Hill Book Company, 1959), pp. 13-15.

25. Margolis, "Demand for Urban Public Services," p. 543. Margolis uses this reasoning to transform merit goods to a general class of public goods for analytical purposes.

26. J.G. Head, "On Merit Goods," *Finanzarchiv* 25, no. 1 (1966): 1-29. See also, J.G. Head, "Public Goods and Public Policy," *Public Finance/Finances Publique* 17, no. 3 (1962): 197-219.

27. Mechanic, *Mental Health*, pp. 25-26.

28. Sloan, *Planning Public Expenditures*, pp. 6-11.

29. See, for example, Katona and Mueller, *Consumer Behavior*. See also, Grover Wirick and Robin Barlow, "Social and Economic Determinants of the Demand for Health Services," in Conference on the Economics of Health and Medical Care, *The Economics of Health and Medical Care: Proceedings* (Ann Arbor: University of Michigan Press, 1962).

30. W. Bolman and J. Westman, "Prevention of Mental Disorder: An Overview of Current Programs," *American Journal of Psychiatry* 123 (March 1967): 1058-68.

31. Margolis, "Demand for Urban Public Services," p. 560.

32. Ibid.

33. "Metropolitan Finance Reconsidered," pp. 412-417.

34. W.A. Hirsch, "Local vs. Areawide Urban Government Services," *National Tax Journal* 27, no. 4 (1964): 331-39.

35. Samuelson, "Public Expenditure Theories."

36. "Metropolitan Finance Reconsidered."

37. Margolis, "Demand for Urban Public Services," p. 543.

38. Both equity and equal access have several definitions. For a discussion, see Cotton M. Lindsay, "Medical Care and the Economics of Sharing," *Economica* N.S. 36, no. 144 (1969): 351-62.

39. Bernard J. Frieden and James Peters, "Urban Planning and Health Services: Opportunities for Cooperation," *Journal of the American Institute of Planners* 36 (March 1970): 82-95; and Sloan, "Planning Public Expenditures," p. 13.

40. Margolis, "Demand for Urban Public Services," p. 541, and pp. 532-33.

41. "Metropolitan Finance Reconsidered."

42. For a discussion of popular stress induced by observing people who are suffering from mental illness, see J. Grad and P. Sainbury, "Evaluating the

Community Psychiatric Service in Chichester," *Milbank Memorial Fund Quarterly* 44 (January 1966): 246-77.

43. Margolis, "Demand for Urban Public Services," pp. 542-43.

Notes to Chapter 5
Westside Mental Health Center — A Case Study

1. *The Social Order of the Slum,* pp. 3-15; Robert E. Park, Ernest W. Burgess, and Roderick D. McKenzie, *The City* (Chicago: University of Chicago Press, 1967).

2. E. Shevsky and W. Bell, "Social Area Analysis," in G. Theodorson, *Studies in Human Ecology* (New York: Row, Peterson, 1961), pp. 226-35; W. Bell, "The Utility of the Shevsky Typology in the Design of Urban Sub-Area Field Studies," in Theodorson, *Studies* pp. 244-52; D. Hawley and O. Duncan, "Social Area Analysis: A Critical Appraisal," *Land Economics Journal,* 33, no. 4 (November 1957): 337-44.

Notes to Chapter 6
Analysis of Consumer Behavior with Respect to Attributes
of Clients and of Services Provided by Westside Mental
Health Center

1. John H. Mueller, Karl F. Schuessler, and Herbert L. Costner, *Statistical Reasoning in Sociology,* 2nd ed. (Boston: Houghton-Mifflin Co., 1970), pp. 249, 257; W. Allen Wallis and Harry V. Roberts, *Statistics: A New Approach* (Glencoe, Ill.: Free Press, 1956), p. 280.

2. S. Siegel, *Nonparametric Statistics for the Behavior Sciences* (New York: McGraw-Hill Book Co., 1956), p. 178; Theodore R. Anderson and Morris Zelditch, Jr., *A Basic Course in Statistics with Sociological Applications,* 2nd ed. (New York: Holt, Rinehart and Winston, 1968), pp. 261-62.

3. J. Galtung, *Theory and Methods of Social Research* (New York: Columbia University Press, 1967), p. 225.

4. This approach is similar to the eight-step methodology for hypothesis construction and testing described by Denzin in his essay, "The Social Survey and Its Variations," in Norman K. Denzin (ed.), *Sociological Methods* (Chicago: Aldine Publishing Co., 1970), pp. 206-207.

5. The psychiatric role of churches for several groups and of spiritualist "folk psychotherapists" for Puerto Ricans is discussed in Research Division, Lincoln Hospital Community Mental Health Center, *Anthropological Studies of the Community* (New York: The Center, undated). (Processed.)

6. See the description of the outpatient health facility for members of Amalgomated Clothing Workers in, Office of Program Planning and Education, National Institute of Mental Health, *The Mental Health of Urban America* (Washington: GPO, 1969), p. 90.

7. A more extensive treatment of techniques for disseminating information which would influence self-referrals, based on the data assembled for this study, is provided in Kathy M. Van Ness, "Diffusion of Information as a Strategy in Urban Planning: The Case of Referral Sources for Mental Health Services," (Masters thesis, University of Washington, 1973).

Notes to Chapter 8
The Influence of Type and Delivery of Clinical Services
on the Behavior of Westside Mental Health Center
Clients

1. Nathan Caplan, "Treatment Intervention and Reciprocal Interaction Effects," *Journal of Social Issues* 24, no. 1 (1968): 63-88.

2. Ginzberg et al., *Urban Health Services*, p. 230.

3. Frieden and Peters, "Urban Planning," p. 90.

Notes to Chapter 9
Suggestions for Further Research

1. Bernard J. Frieden, "The Changing Prospects for Social Planning," *Journal of the American Institute of Planners* 33 (September 1967): 318; Herbert J. Gans, "Planning–and City Planning–for Mental Health," in H. Wentworth Eldredge (ed.), *Taming Megalopolis,* vol. 2 (Garden City, N.Y.: Doubleday and Company, 1967), pp. 897-916; Britton Harris, "The Uses of Theory in the Simulation of Urban Phenomena," *Journal of the American Institute of Planners* 32 (September 1966): 258-72.

2. See especially Kevin J. Lancaster, "A New Approach to Consumer Theory," *Journal of Political Economy* 74, no. 2 (1966): 132-57. Lancaster cites Johnson's skeptical paraphrase of the conclusion of consumer theory; that a good is a good. Harry Johnson, "Demand Theory Further Revised, or Goods are Goods," *Economica* N.S. 25 (May 1958).

3. Hagen similarly conceives of these features as "elements of usefulness." Ole Hagen, "Elements of Value," *Stahphommisk Tidsskrift* 81 (1967): 39-51.

4. Lancaster, "New Approach," p. 134.

5. The postulated consumption technology is directly analogous to Leontief's input-output formulation of production technology. Lancaster, "New

Approach," pp. 137-42; Hagen, "Elements of Value," pp. 45-47; Kevin Lancaster, "Change and Innovation in the Technology of Consumption," *American Economic Review* 56 (1966): 14-23; and comments by Hans Blems, ibid., pp. 43-45.

6. Lancaster, "New Approach," pp. 154-55.

7. Richard Quandt and William Baumol, "The Demand for Abstract Transport Modes: Theory and Measurement," *Journal of Regional Science* 6, no. 2 (1966), pp. 13-26.

8. For a critical response, stressing the problems of interpreting and statistically testing the log-linear formulation used by Quandt and Baumol, see Reuben Gronau and Roger Alcaly, "The Demand for Abstract Transport Modes: Some Misgivings," *Journal of Regional Science* 9, no. 1 (1969): 153-57. See also the rejoinder and additional references by Quandt and Baumol, "The Demand for Abstract Transport Modes: Some Hopes," ibid., pp. 159-62.

9. William Baumol, "Caluculation of Optimal Product and Retailer Characteristics: The Abstract Product Approach," *Journal of Political Economy* 75, no. 5 (1967): 674-85.

10 Edward A. Suchman, "Social Patterns of Illness and Medical Care," *Journal of Health and Human Behavior* 6 (Spring 1965). Miller and Mishler point out that the kind of psychiatric treatment administered is also associated with the client's position in the class structure. "Social Class, Mental Illness, and American Psychiatry: An Expository Review," *Milbank Memorial Fund Quarterly* 37 (April 1959): 174-99.

11. S. Manning, "Cultural and Value Factors Affecting the Negro's Use of Agency Services," *Social Work* 5 (1960): 3-13.

12. L.Y. Kline, "Some Factors in the Psychiatric Treatment of Spanish-Americans," *American Journal of Psychiatry* 125 (June 1969): 1674-81. See also, J. Kennedy, "Problems Posed in the Analysis of Negro Patients," *Psychiatry* 15 (1952): 313-27.

13. Leopold Bellak, "The Comprehensive Community Psychiatry Program in City Hospital," in Bellak (ed.), *Handbook of Community Psychiatry and Community Mental Health* (New York: Grune and Stratton, 1964), pp. 144-65; Peter Rogatz and Marge Rogatz, "Role For The Consumer," *Social Policy*, 1 (January/February 1971): 52-56.

14. T. Linn, "Social Characteristics and Social Interaction in the Utilization of a Psychiatric Outpatient Clinic," *Journal of Health and Social Behavior* 8 (March 1967): 3-14; R. Coles, "Racial Problems in Psychotherapy," *Current Psychiatric Therapy* 6 (1966): 110-113.

15. This tactic proved especially effective at neighborhood service centers operated by Lincoln Hospital in New York City. E. Hallowitz and F. Riessman, "The Role of the Indigenous Nonprofessional in a Community Mental Health

Neighborhood Service Center Program," *American Journal of Orthopsychiatry* 37 (July 1967): 766-78. The stress on nonprofessionals stemming from filling dual roles is discussed by P. Levinson and J. Schiller, "Role Analysis of the Indigenous Nonprofessional," *Social Work* 11 (July 1966): 95-101. See also, Arthur Pearl and Frank Riessman, *New Carrers for the Poor: The Nonprofessional in Human Service* (New York: Free Press, 1965).

16. Frank Riessman, "The New Approach to the Poor," in Milton Greenblatt, Paul E. Emery, and Bernard C. Glueck (eds.), *Poverty and Mental Health,* Psychiatric Research Report No. 21 (Washington: American Psychiatric Association, 1967), pp. 40-42. See also, Joseph P. Lyford, *The Airtight Cage: A Study of New York's West Side* (New York: Harper and Row, 1966). Rein also deals with professional domination of service programs, the usefulness of information which consumers can provide directly to the design and management process, and the desirability of restructuring incentives to make services responsible and resonsive to consumers. Martin Rein, *Social Policy: Issues of Choice and Change* (New York: Random House, 1970).

17. D.J. Scherl and J.T. English, "Community Mental Health and Comprehensive Health Service Programs for the Poor," *American Journal of Psychiatry* 125 (June 1969): 1666-74.

18. See. F.S. Chapin, Jr., and Thomas H. Logan, "Patterns of Time and Space Use," in Harvey Perloff (ed.), *The Quality of the Urban Environment* (Washington: Resources for the Future, 1969), pp. 305-332; F.S. Chapin, Jr., "Activity Systems and Urban Structure: A Working Scheme," *Journal of the American Institute of Planners* 34 (January 1968): 11-18.

19. Gerald F. Jacobson, "Crisis Theory and Treatment Strategy: Some Socio-Cultural and Psychodynamic Considerations," *Journal of Neuroses and Mental Disorders* 141 (August 1965): 209-218.

20. Robert Sommer, *Personal Space, The Behavioral Basis of Design* (Englewood Cliffs, N.J.: Prentice-Hall, 1969), esp. pp. 77-97; Jerome S. Bruner et al., "Expectation and the Perception of Color," *American Journal of Psychology* 64 (April 1951): 216-27.

21. E.A. Clark, "Community Care," *Progressive Architecture* (February 1969), pp. 93-103.

22. See Herbert Gans, *People and Plans,* pp. 179-80. Steinitz cites the role of design in facilitating use and avoiding frustration, and found little difference in response to design features based on social class. Carl Steinitz, "Meaning and the Congruence of Urban Form and Activity," *Journal of the American Institute of Planners* (July 1968): 233-48. Schorr's review of the sociological literature on housing unit design reaches the same conclusion, except for upper-middle-class people who show substantial interest and have training in design. Alvin L. Schorr, *Slums and Social Insecurity,* U.S. Dept. of Health, Education, and Welfare Research Report No. 1 (Washington: GPO, 1966). The symbolic

meaning of buildings or their associations can also have an impact on utilization. For example, the Chinese community in the central area of San Francisco regard San Francisco General Hospital as a place to which people go to die. It is widely thought that this contributes to their reticence to use the outpatient clinic which is located in the hospital complex.

23. William Baumol and Edward Ide discuss the positive role of size, in terms of number of functions or services, until scale exerts a diseconomy in terms of high shopping costs and declining marginal value. "Variety in Retailing," *Management Science* 3 (October 1956): 95-96. See also, David Stea and Raymond G. Studer, "Architectural Programming, Environmental Design, and Human Behavior," *Journal of Social Issues* 22 (1966): 127-36.

24. Alis D. Runge, "The Health Megacenter," *Progressive Architecture* (February 1968), pp. 110-117.

25. Karl Kansky, "Travel Patterns of Urban Residents," *Transportation Science* 1 (November 1967): 261-85. Availability of transportation will also play a significant role in the time-distance cost faced by a prospective client. See "Race and the Urban Transportation Problem," in J.R. Meyer, J.F. Kain, and M. Wohl, *The Urban Transportation Problem* (Cambridge: Harvard University Press, 1965), pp. 144-67.

26. Samuel A. Stouffer, "Intervening Opportunities: A Theory Relating Mobility and Distance," *American Sociological Review* 5 (1940): 845-67.

27. Jens Kofoed, "Person Movement Research: A Discussion of Concepts," *Papers of the Regional Science Association* 24 (1970): 141-55; R.G. Golledge, "Conceptualizing the Market Decision Process," *Journal of Regional Science* (Winter 1967). See also, Christen T. Jonassen, "Relationship of Attitudes and Behavior in Ecological Mobility," *Social Forces* 34 (October 1955): 64-67.

28. Kofoed, "Person Movement Research," pp. 147-48.

29. Several authors have made the case for outpatient services provided within acceptable walking distance, especially for clients who for various reasons have limited physical mobility. See, for example, Robert Perlman, "Social Welfare Planning and Physical Planning," *Journal of the American Institute of Planners* 32 (July 1966) : 237-41; Frieden and Peters, "Urban Planning," p. 87; Scherl and English, "Community Mental Health," p. 1673; Emmanuel Hallowitz, "The Role of a Neighborhood Center in Community Mental Health," *American Journal of Orthopsychiatry* 38 (July 1968): 705–714.

30. Edward T. Hall, "Human Needs and Inhuman Cities," *Smithsonian Annual* 2 (1968): 163-72. Hägerstrand, "What About People in Regional Science," *Papers of the Regional Science Association* 24 (1970).

31. Kofoed, "Person Movement Research," p. 154; Roger N. Shepard, "The Analysis of Proximities: Multidimensional Scaling with an Unknown Distance Function," *Psychometrika* 27 (1962): 129-40 and 219-46.

32. See, for example, Daniel Rosenblatt and Edward Suchman, "Awareness

of Physician's Social Status in the Washington Heights Master Sample Survey," *Milbank Memorial Fund Quarterly* 37, no. 1 (1969): 94-102.

33. Toaru Ishiyama, "The Mental Hospital Patient-Consumer as a Determinant of Service," *Mental Hygiene* 54 (April 1970): 221-29.

34. Quandt and Baumol, "Demand for Abstract Transport Modes: Theory and Measurement."

35. Ibid., p. 19.

36. Quandt and Baumol, "Demand for Abstract Transport Modes: Some Hopes," p. 160.

37. J.P. Mayberry, *Variants of Abstract Mode Models,* Mathematica Working Paper No. 1006 (Princeton: Mathematica, July 1968).

38. See Quandt and Baumol, "Demand for Abstract Transport Modes: Some Hopes," p. 161.

39. Ibid., p. 17.

40. Richard E. Quandt and Kan Hua Young, "Cross-Sectional Travel Models: Estimates and Tests," *Journal of Regional Science* 9 (August 1969): 201-214.

41. Morrill and Earickson, "Character and Use of Chicago Area Hospitals"; and "Locational Efficiency."

Index

About the Author

Donald Harlan Miller is associate professor of urban planning at the University of Washington. He received the Ph.D. in city and regional planning from the University of California at Berkeley in 1972. Dr. Miller's current research interests include development and application of disaggregated consumer demand analysis in designing and evaluating local public services; investigation of intraregional locational behavior of residential units and commercial establishments, for refining current theories of urban spatial structure; and design and application of program evaluation systems, with emphasis on output and goal achievement measures, and on feasible methods of valuating goals. He is the author of numerous articles and papers concerning urban planning.

DATE DUE

MAY 04
